# THE Incredible POWER OF Grace

## Roland R. Hegstad

When God's
Assurance
Becomes
Your
Own

REVIEW AND HERALD® PUBLISHING ASSOCIATION
HAGERSTOWN, MD 21740

The author assumes full responsibility for the accuracy of all facts and
quotations as cited in this book.

This book was
Copyedited by Delma Miller and James Cavil
Edited by Tim Crosby
Cover designed by square1studio
Cover art by It Is Written Digital Media Group/Darrin Brooks
Typeset: 11/12 Bembo

PRINTED IN U.S.A.

09  08  07  06  05          5  4  3  2  1

**R&H Cataloging Service**
Hegstad, Roland R
The incredible power of grace: when God's assurance becomes your own

    1. Salvation    I. Title

        234

ISBN 0-8280-1912-6

# Dedication

To my wife, Stella, who has inspired me
to explore ever deeper dimensions of love.

Other books by Roland R. Hegstad:
*Nobody's Boy*
*Who Causes Suffering?*

# Contents

## Chapter 1

# MAP OF A TENDER PERSON

She was born to money, this slim girl with the strangely haunted eyes. Her name was Pegeen. Call her the "Champagne Girl," for she was of vintage stock. Picture her against a velvet backdrop of high-society debutante balls, jet-set parties, opening night at the Met, dinner at the Stork Club. She wintered in Florida, summered in Paris, and called the servants occasionally to learn at which home her mother was in residence. Her mother was Peggy Guggenheim, American millionaire and patron of the arts. Pegeen was brilliant and talented. Even in her 20s she was gaining recognition as an artist of promise. When I met her, she lived in Paris, at a luxury hotel on an island in the middle of the Seine. There, in her private studio, she painted. Her strange, dark-hued compositions troubled me, for they seemed in some strange way to reveal something hidden far beneath her fleeting smiles.

By most criteria Pegeen was a success. She had tasted life at its frothy best. But it left her strangely desolate. Friends found her body among empty barbiturate bottles and tubes of paint at the foot of her last painting. On its gloomy surface she had depicted the dismal paths people take in search of love. All led to death. She had titled it *Map of a Tender Person*.

7

He was a railroad magnate, a man of exceptional drive and ambition, with not only the capacity to achieve but also the drive to excel. Robert Ralph Young became one of the most powerful railroad tycoons of our day. He collected all the prizes of a champion—wealth, power, influence, palatial homes in Palm Beach and Newport. There were, to be sure, temporary setbacks, self-doubts. After one period of introspection, he wrote a poem. In a sense it was his map of a tender person:

> Until today it seemed my path led upward,
> But now I find myself upon a constant downward
> slope
> Which gains in pitch until I see
> Dim, distantly, a void,
> From which departed friends have vainly turned
> tired faces,
> And love has lost its zest,
> The quest of fortune ended.

Still he acquired things. But man cannot live by things alone. So one day Robert Young sat despondently in a chair, carefully positioned a double-barreled 20-gauge shotgun between his knees, put the barrels against his head, and pulled both triggers.

Of all his things, in the end, what did he save for himself?

Two 20-gauge shotgun shells.

A beautiful actress dined one night in a famous restaurant in Malibu Beach, California. She was fearfully insecure, often breaking into tears and hives from nervousness. It took her six hours to make up for her part in the movie *Gentlemen Prefer Blondes*. Before she left the restaurant, she was asked to sign the guest register. She wrote her sex goddess name:

Marilyn Monroe. She hesitated for a moment over her address, and at last wrote: "Nowhere." The next day she tried once again to find her identity in pills and alcohol, as she had been doing for months. She died that day, never knowing who she really was.

Call her Karen. No security in her home. Parents divorced; remarriage no improvement.

Karen left for college with the honest intention of facing up to herself, her inner conflicts, her emptiness. A plain young woman, Karen two-toned her hair, silvered her toes, and slicked her lips with translucent pink. As the cliché goes: "It pays to advertise." The males got the message. Several were willing to make her feel as if she really "belonged."

When she got pregnant, she slipped off to the justice of the peace with the young man most likely to be the father. The tragedy is that today Karen's needs are still unmet. In fact, they are compounded. She wonders now whether he ever really loved her, or ever will. Increasingly she suspects that so far as he is concerned, she is just another set of "vital statistics." And good statistics are a dime a dozen in these fad-diet days. Haunting her is the question of what his attitude will be when she comes to resemble a literal pear more than the figurative "peach" she now is. Then it will matter, matter deeply, she now realizes, whether he loves her for the lovely person she believes herself to be deep down inside.

Rex was a painfully insecure youth, so scrawny that when he turned sideways, he disappeared. His childhood in Wauna, Oregon, was haunted by the disintegrating relationship between his father and mother. Etched indelibly on his memory was the night his drunken father was hunting for his .32 automatic to kill his wife and two children. Terrified, Rex ran from the house into knee-deep snow and huddled against the roots of a fallen tree. He could hear his mother's screams and his little sister's cries. Though raised in a nonreligious home, he prayed his first prayer that night, sobbing a plea heavenward: "Please, God, don't let Daddy kill us! Please, God, please . . ."

There were better times. Rex excelled in school. A perceptive teacher encouraged his talents in writing and art. But somewhere, deep down inside, was an emptiness. Long matured beyond his childhood prayer, he scoffed at religion and despised ministers. And then something happened . . .

## How to Measure Happiness

Real living, it seems, is not just things—money, clothes, yachts. Nor is life just parties, liquor, a good time, drugs, sex. There's a reason: We are not just bodies. We are three-dimensional beings—physical, mental, spiritual. We need material things—food, clothing, shelter—but satisfying these needs will not in itself bring happiness. Jesus pointed this out when He said, "Man shall not live by bread alone" (Matthew 4:4). Something more is needed, including love, belonging, success, security, a sense of personal worth, recognition as a person. Psychologists agree that no amount of material things, no amount of physical pleasure, will quiet the hunger pangs of unfulfilled needs. Only when both our physical and higher needs are met can we enjoy happiness in all its dimensions.

In Rod McKuen's poem "Something More," a young man walks all the roads there are to life, sees all there is to see, and dares death in order to pursue life. Five stanzas of the six-stanza poem conclude with the words "There must be something more." The last line ends, "God, but there must be something more!"

The Bible pictures God, who made us, seeking to meet our highest needs. Jesus once said, "Behold the fowls of the air: . . . your heavenly Father feedeth them. Are ye not much better than they? . . . Consider the lilies of the field, how they grow; . . . even Solomon in all his glory was not arrayed like one of these. . . . Shall he not much more clothe you, O ye of little faith? Therefore take no [anxious] thought, saying, What shall we eat? or, What shall we drink? or, Wherewithal shall we be clothed? . . . But seek ye first the kingdom of God, and his righteousness; and all these things shall be added unto you" (Matthew 6:26-33).

Unfortunately, we are at war with a skilled and unprincipled enemy. And booty is his bait.

The apostle Paul warned: "We are up against the unseen power that controls this dark world, and . . . agents from the very headquarters of evil" (Ephesians 6:12, Phillips). This unseen evil force—traditionally known as Lucifer, or Satan—concentrates on keeping us blissfully unaware of the happiness God offers. He promotes ersatz satisfactions, enticing us with physical pleasure when we could have love, seducing us with material goods when we could have true success. He tempts us to meet legitimate needs—yearnings God Himself created in us—in an illegitimate way that is contrary to the laws of our being. He tempts us to carry to excess that which is, in itself, lawful. And these things destroy our happiness.

Let's look at a case from Bible days. Name unknown. Male. About 40 years old. Lacked a sense of worth. Suffered from palsy. Doctors of today who have examined his case history say his problem likely began in his mind.

Maybe his parents were to blame. Call a chair ugly, and nothing happens to it. Even if it's a Chippendale, it just sits there, neither insulted nor embarrassed. But call a child ugly or stupid or clumsy often enough, vehemently enough, and she will come to believe it. Stamped on the mental map of a tender person is the conviction that he is stupid. She is clumsy. He gives up on himself, believing that safety lies in not trying. Her life motto becomes "If I don't try, I can't fail."

The religious leaders of his day wanted nothing to do with this man. They thought his sickness was God's punishment for his sins; he got just what he deserved.

Then one day friends brought him to Jesus.

How does one describe the healing look of this God-man? I can't. I believe that Jesus' look penetrated deeply into the man's mind and read there the record of his life—his failures, his needs. Jesus spoke to him: "Son . . ."

The sick man raises his head wonderingly. Son? He would claim me—ugly me, stupid me, sinful me, worthless me—as son?

A flush of hope tints his cheeks. Son? Me?

"Yes, you. Son, your sins are forgiven" (see Mark 2:5, TEV). Why did Jesus say this before adding "Get up, pick up your mat, and walk"? Perhaps He was using a familiar form of address. Or perhaps He had diagnosed a deep need and ministered to it. On one point the Bible leaves no doubt: the man recovered.

Many people are so tormented by their failures and sins that their sense of worth is gone, their hope destroyed. Sometimes the body too is affected. Doctors tell us that many of today's diseases may have their origin in a troubled conscience. Whatever our need, the words of a loving Savior are for us: "Son, Daughter, your sins are forgiven. Take up your bed and walk."

What difference does it make how we live? Paul answered that question: "It is time to wake up to reality. . . . The night is nearly over, the day [of Christ's return] has almost dawned. Let us therefore fling away the things that men do in the dark, let us arm ourselves for the fight of the day! Let us live cleanly, as in the daylight, not in the delights of getting drunk or playing with sex, nor yet in quarreling or jealousies. Let us be Christ's men from head to foot, and give no chances to the flesh to have its fling" (Romans 13:11-14, Phillips).

There you have it: Pegeen. Robert Ralph Young. The victim of palsy. Karen. Case histories of God's offers and Satan's alternatives.

It's time to wake up to reality. It's never too late to start over. It's never too late to begin to enjoy life in its fullness, as God intended.

One of the most beautiful stories in the Bible—in fact, in all literature—is that of Gomer and Hosea (Hosea 1-3). Gomer, the wife, left Hosea and their children for another man. For years she lived in luxury. Then—her health ruined, her physical bank account overdrawn, no man willing to have her—she was put on the auction block to be sold as a slave to the highest bidder.

See her there, head bowed in hopelessness. A circle of men stand about her. They know what she is. She hears their coarse comments. Then—silence! The circle parts, and through it strides a man. A whisper slinks around the circle: "It's Hosea. Hosea! It's her husband."

Come to mock her? to shame her? to remind her of spurned love? That would be justice. But Hosea comes when no man will have her, when sin is done with her, and buys her back. Takes her home. And loves her again as his wife.

Hosea is like Jesus Christ. Gomer is like us. Hosea—Christ—came when sin was done with us, when we'd been "had," when no sane being in all the universe could stand to be in our presence, and bought us back!

If only someone could have gotten that message to Pegeen before she finished her last painting, *Map of a Tender Person*.

When my wife, Stella, and I were at our son's home in Loma Linda a few months ago, he got a video he wanted us to see. It was titled *Mr. Holland's Opus*—opus being the singular for opera.

Filmed at Grant High School in Portland, it's the story of an aspiring musician who has to take a temporary job teaching music appreciation in a local high school. He doesn't really want to be there. He wants to pursue his dream of composing a piece of great American music. But his wife, Iris, is expecting a child. So Mr. Holland puts aside his dreams and takes up the everyday realities of teaching tone-deaf students to make music.

Over the years Mr. Holland comes to love his job teaching kids the beauty and the power of music. His contagious passion even manages to get through to a few of them, and his music lifts them out of their broken circumstances.

And then, in the blink of an eye, 30 years have passed. There's a budget crunch, and the principal tells him that the school can get by without music. "You work all your life," he tells a friend. "You think what you do is important to people. Then you wake up and find you're expendable."

As the film nears its end, we see Holland, now 62, sitting in an empty music room. Even the racks are devoid of music. His son and wife come to help him carry the last boxes home. Passing the auditorium, he hears music, as if instruments are being tuned. He opens the door to see what's going on. The auditorium is packed with students and parents. They stand and cheer as he is ushered to a seat in front.

A minute later the door swings open again. The

governor strides in. Governor Gertrude Lang. The little red-haired girl from his music appreciation class—the lone underachiever in a family in which everyone else excelled. Gertrude Lang, who couldn't master the clarinet—until he took the sheet music away and told her simply to play her dream.

She comes to the platform, quiets the cheering students and parents and teachers, and speaks.

"Glenn Holland, you probably are thinking that you're a failure. You didn't achieve your dream. But you've had a profound influence on my life and many more. Not a life in this room has been untouched by you.

"You have a symphony, Glenn Holland. We are your symphony. The melody and the notes of your opus. We are the music of your life."

And Gertrude Lang, the girl who couldn't play a note, takes her place in the orchestra, behind a sign reading "Class of '65," picks up her clarinet, and waits for Glenn Holland to raise his baton and bring forth the music he instilled in the souls of his students.

One thing I learned from this movie is that life has meaning when you are making meaning for someone else. But indulge me an allegorical look at the tale for a moment. If Glenn Holland is a little bit like God (He was rejected too), then do you know what that makes you?

You are God's opus.

You are part of His great symphony. You may be a missing part. You may be out of tune, underplayed, and more than slightly off-key. You may have been absent from your seat in the orchestra for a long time. But God's got a place for you. He wrote you into His score.

There's a passage in Jeremiah 29:11-13 that explains how He feels about you. " 'For I know the plans I have for you,' declares the Lord, 'plans to prosper you and not to harm you, plans to give you hope and a future. Then you will call upon me and come and pray to me, and I will listen to you. You will seek me and find me when you seek me with all your heart'" (NIV).

Does God really care about you? Does He actually have plans for your life? Let me tell you a true story.

One Sabbath morning my wife, Stella, and our youngest daughter, Kimberly, were seated in the second row of a large church in Takoma Park, Maryland. As we stood to sing the morning hymn, a young soldier in uniform saw an empty seat just beyond us and with a whispered apology slipped past. I glanced at him—five eight, curly hair, and blue eyes—and assumed he was a soldier stationed at Walter Reed Hospital. After the service we stepped out into the aisle and joined the hundreds headed for dinner.

Suddenly a voice spoke to me. "Go back and speak to the soldier."

Now, spoken messages from God are definitely not an everyday affair. *It can't be,* I thought, and turned toward the door. Again the voice: "Go back and speak to the soldier." I turned and saw him standing near the front of the church looking at the stained-glass windows. Puzzled by the message, but recognizing that the Holy Spirit directly or through an angel was communicating with me, I made my way back to the soldier and introduced myself. I quickly learned John was a visitor. "I saw your church a week ago and thought I'd come by to see how you worship," he said.

"Well, John, why don't you come home with us for dinner, and see how we eat?"

So it was that we were soon sitting on our living room sofa and getting acquainted while my wife, who had not expected company, whipped up some extra salad.

After lunch (John loved the salad and left with the recipe) we returned to the sofa. His primary concern, I found, was whether he had ever really been baptized. He told me that he had, according to the rites of his parents' church, been sprinkled as a baby.

"Turn to John 3:23," I suggested, "and read it to me."

John read: " 'Now John [the Baptist] also was baptizing in Aenon near Salim, because there was much water there' " (NKJV).

"Why did John go to Aenon to baptize?" I asked.

"Because there was much water there."

"If baptism could be done out of a teacup, why would John go where there was "much water"?

"I never thought of that," John replied.

"Now," I said, "let's go to the book of Romans, chapter 6. Here we find that what baptism symbolizes cannot be achieved by a teacup of water."

" 'Do you not know that as many of us as were baptized into Christ Jesus were baptized into His death? Therefore we were buried with Him through baptism into death, that just as Christ was raised from the dead by the glory of the Father, even so we also should walk in newness of life' (verses 3, 4, NKJV).

"John, I want you to notice that only baptism by immersion can truly convey the spiritual lessons God wishes to communicate. When we are baptized, we figuratively die with Christ, are buried with Him—by immersion—and then are raised from the [watery] grave, even as He was. You can't convey these wonderful truths by sprinkling a bit of water on someone's head!"

Two months later, after further study together, I baptized John in the baptistry of my church. As we drove to a friend's home afterward, John pulled out his diary.

"I thought you might like to see what I wrote in my diary just one month before meeting you in the church."

He handed it to me, and I read: "Dear Lord, I am

troubled over baptism. I'm not sure I was ever really baptized. Please, if I should be baptized by immersion, send someone to help me find that truth."

He had erased something, and I asked him what he had written.

"Well, if I were to be baptized," he said, "I asked the Lord to let the one who brought me that truth baptize me. Then I thought maybe I was being presumptuous, so I erased that part."

I sat, silent and meditative. What if I had not heeded the voice of God and returned to meet John? It was not just his future that was at stake. Within the next few months John's mother (his father was dead) and sister and her husband were baptized—by immersion, of course.

When John was looking for God, he discovered that God was looking for him. God cared enough about him to reach out and touch one of His servants by the name of Rex—that's me—and put him on John's trail. Yes, I'm the painfully insecure youth who begged God not to let his dad shoot his mom. Rex is my middle name. I'd rather be called Roland. It's only fair to tell you that once upon a time I had no use for religion. I grew up disrespecting all institutional religion. In fact, you won't get far in this book before you will learn what this world would be like if I were God! I despised ministers. But—would you believe?—I became one.

I never wanted to be a minister. I wanted to be a sports editor, thrilling to sports scores rather than to the status of the Big Game up there! But God had dreamed His own dream about me. And His dream became mine.

As a young minister I still had a lot to learn. I used to measure my service by the number of people I could convince of church doctrine. Still, I trusted in words, my words, polysyllabic profundity, rather than the Word. And then about the time I thought I was producing an epic opus, the Lord convicted me that my symphony was nothing more than "sounding brass or a clanging cymbal." Useless cacophony.

God showed me that doctrine means nothing unless we have experienced a spiritual "resurrection" through the new birth. Choosing the right day of rest means nothing unless we are resting in Him. Knowing about righteousness by faith means nothing if we are not exercising faith through loving service.

After weeks of prayers and tears light penetrated the darkness of my night, and for the first time in my ministry I could share in the harmony of Christ's love song to His Father: "I delight to do thy will, O my God: yea, thy law is within my heart" (Psalm 40:8).

Today I pray:

"Great Master, touch me with Thy skillful hand;
Let not the music that is in me die!
Great Sculptor, hew and polish me; nor let,
Hidden and lost, Thy form within me lie!
Spare not the stroke! Do with me as Thou wilt!
Let there be naught unfinished, broken, marred;
Complete Thy purpose that I may become
Thy perfect image, Thou my God and Lord!"
—Horatius Bonar

God cares about you just as much as He cared about John. Or me. He has dreams for you, too. The very fact that you're reading this book tells me you are searching. Well, God was searching for you a long time ago. The good news is—you're found! And you're about to find the hope and the glorious future that God has for you.

## Chapter 2

# IF I
# WERE GOD

During my high school years I was unconvinced that there was a God. But I had pretty well formulated concepts of how things would be if I were God! What would I do? First off, employees of the IRS would all be out playing golf. Those top guns of industry who fire 10,000 or 20,000 workers to increase company profits while they draw salaries of $10 million or $20 million a year would all be saying "Anything else, sir?" from behind a counter at McDonald's.

If I were God, believe me, things would be different in church. Sermons would get interesting for a change, or—ZAP, and a new preacher would be behind the pulpit. Maybe I'd get rid of pulpits. Just have a debating society. Or I'd replace hymnals with buttons: press 1, and you change the sermon to something more comfortable. Press 2, and you cut five minutes off the sermon. Press 3, and the sermon disappears. Press 4, and the preacher disappears. Press 5, and the Holy Spirit may show up.

And if I were God, things would be different outside of church too. A lot of wrongs would get righted really quick! Terrorists and road hogs and that nasty salesperson I just met would all get their come-uppance. If I were God, pretty soon the only people left walking around free would be nice people.

Like me.

But since *God* is God—well, sometimes He seems a bit lax. Consider the story of the prodigal son Jesus told to illustrate God's forgiving grace. The young man tells his father to give him his share of the family fortune so he can "really live." If he'd been my son and returned home broke, you can bet I wouldn't have greeted that womanizer with a beefsteak dinner. Never! Send him to the barn to live with the camels! Make him a servant! That would be justice!

But God chose another option. Martha Snell Nicholson describes it in poetic verse:

I sinned. And straightway, posthaste, Satan flew
Before the presence of the Most High God,
And made a railing accusation there.
He said, "This soul, this thing of clay and sod,
Has sinned. 'Tis true that he has named Thy name,

"But I demand his death, for Thou hast said,
  'The soul that sinneth, it shall die.' Shall not
  Thy sentence be fulfilled? Is justice dead?
  Send now this wretched sinner to his doom.
  What other thing can a righteous ruler do?"
And thus he did accuse me day and night
And every word he spoke, O God, was true!

Then quickly One rose up from God's right hand,
Before whose glory angels veiled their eyes.
He spoke, "Each jot and tittle of the law
Must be fulfilled; the guilty sinner dies!
But wait—Suppose his guilt were all transferred
To Me, and that I paid his penalty!

"Behold My hands, My side, My feet! One day

I was made sin for him, and died that he
　Might be presented faultless at Thy throne."
And Satan fled away. Full well he knew
That he could not prevail against such love,
For every word my dear Lord spoke was true!

Satan appeared to Christ in the wilderness one day. Weakened by 40 days and nights of fasting, Jesus was famished, with no Taco Bell or McDonald's nearby. "Now when the tempter came to Him, he said, 'If You are the Son of God, command that these stones become bread'" (Matthew 4:2, 3, NKSV).

If it were me, I'd have made bread—whole-wheat, rye, potato bread, raisin bread—and tossed in a few buns for good measure. There wouldn't have been a rock for miles around.

*But then you wouldn't have a Savior!*

Instead, Jesus answered, "It is written, 'Man shall not live by bread alone, but by every word that proceeds from the mouth of God.' Then the devil took Him up into the holy city, set Him on the pinnacle of the temple, and said to Him, 'If You are the Son of God, throw Yourself down. For it is written: "He shall give His angels charge over you," and "In their hands they shall bear you up, lest you dash your foot against a stone"'" (verses 4-6, NKJV).

Provoke me with a challenge like that, and I'd have dived off the pinnacle, looped a few times to show my mastery of gravitation, and come to a gentle stop two inches above the ground.

*And you wouldn't have a Savior!*

It's hard not to be impressed by the restraint of Jesus in using power. To show power, if you've got it, is human. But to show restraint is divine.

"Again, the devil took Him up on an exceedingly high mountain, and showed Him all the kingdoms of the world and their glory. And he said to Him, 'All these things I will give You if You will fall down and worship me'" (verses 8, 9, NKJV).

You know what I'd have done. After falling for the first two temptations, I'd have been in no condition to resist the third.

*And you wouldn't have a Savior.*

Satan would be sitting uncontested on the throne of this world. No way would be open to the mercy seat, where forgiveness is to be found.

But back to our day, where the issues don't seem quite so momentous.

Slip into a seat beside me. We're in a tent meeting in a little logging town in the West. The minister, hardly a walking, talking advertisement for robust manhood, is doing his best to deliver a message from God. But a lumberjack—a big, burly fellow with a fifth in his flask and a fifth in his stomach—is disrupting the meeting. He actually stands up and tells the meager audience what he's going to do to the little minister when he's done with his drivel.

Now, if I were God, I'd lead that little minister out into the alley with that big, burly lumberjack. And while the audience looked on, I'd endow the little man with superhuman strength. I'd empower him to put out his scrawny little left arm and disdainfully lift that 250-pound lumberjack off the ground and flip him backwards into the mud! That would be only the beginning. People would learn that it isn't wise to bully a preacher—especially a little one. The lesson finished, I'd lead the little minister to blow on his bruised fists, disdainfully contemplate the bewildered hulk lying in the mud, and invite the awed crowd to the preacher's next night lecture on the virtues of a vegetarian diet. (On reflection, I'll concede that the little minister might as well forgo his coming sermon, "The Meek Shall Inherit the Earth.")

Want to know what the Lord did? He sent the Holy Spirit to give power, not to the little minister, but to the big message. That lumberjack wept at the altar, and today he himself is a preacher.

Oh marvelous grace of the Father above,
Oh infinite grace of His infinite love;
It melts the stone heart into pliable clay
And banishes night into love's perfect day!

What is a god? Ask a Hindu, and you'll find that there are a number of gods, all with different personalities and perspectives. One generally takes a benevolent view of humanity; another zaps people. When the apostle Paul visited Athens 2,000 years ago—not, in his case, for the Olympic Games—he saw many statues. The Greeks regarded their gods somewhat as glorified humans, with all their foibles and follies. One thing for sure: they didn't want to anger any of the gods by missing one. Paul even saw one statue dedicated to the "unknown" god!

What is the Christian God like? We've discovered that He's gracious and forgiving. But ask His followers to describe Him, and even they get in trouble. Turns out that God is one, but there are really three. Anyone want to volunteer to explain the Trinity? Jesus is God, and He came down and became one of us. He prayed to His Father in heaven, yet in Isaiah 9:6 He—the Messiah—is called "the everlasting Father."

The placard over His cross read: "King of the Jews." But kings don't die on crosses. Kings put people on crosses. He called Himself the "Son of man" but also the Son of God. Maybe gods do walk the earth now and then. The Greeks and Romans thought so. But gods don't hang on crosses.

So what is God really like? Some of His followers claim to be just like Him. Unfortunately, some of those followers have murdered millions in His name, while staining history with blood in their attempt to make others just like them. In fact, the history of persecution is not of bad people trying to make other people bad, but of good people trying to make other people good.

One Christian celebrity says God zapped her little poodle because it was piddling on her draperies. Isn't it nice to know that while God is busy zapping heretics in Iraq and Iran and Afghanistan He still has time to deliver one of His saints from a piddling poodle? A poet calls Him the God of "pots and pans and things." Why didn't He just donate a pot for Tammy's poodle?

Or maybe this is not what the real God is like after all. When disciples James and John got all hot and bothered because some disrespectful Samaritans didn't set a banquet for Jesus when He came to their town, they suggested that the Lord empower them to "command fire to come down from heaven, and consume them, even as Elijah did" (Luke 9:54). Jesus rebuked them by suggesting they didn't really understand what spirit was motivating them. "The Son of Man has not come to destroy men's lives," He said, "but to save them" (verse 56, margin, TLB). It appears, then, that God's disciples themselves have at times badly misrepresented Him. No wonder we have a hard time determining what God is really like!

What sort of God would He be if He were really like you and me?

Well, if I were God, you'd know it—as in the comics, when a finger comes out of the clouds, lightning flashes, and we see sinners as a smoldering heap of groveling humanity. I wouldn't stand for anyone misrepresenting my benevolent nature! Say you're on the Beltway. A sign says, "Left lane only for Wheaton turnoff." You're edging into the left lane when a car full of teenagers cuts in front of you—right on your radiator.

Zap!

Now, a zap is a diluted zot. When you zot people, their earthly pilgrimage is over. If I were God, I'd save this for the big stage stuff. The Emmy Awards of Evil—say, for Saddam Hussein.

Pound nails through my hands, put me up on a cross, and if I were God, the whole Middle East would become radioactive waste. "Father, forgive them"? More like Father, forget them! *Gods* don't hang on crosses. Gods hang *people* on crosses.

But God's children hung Him up between the heaven He left and the earth He made. "It is finished!" Jesus cried from the cross. "The great dragon was hurled down—that ancient serpent called the devil, or Satan, who leads the whole world astray. He was hurled to the earth, and his angels with him. Then I heard a loud voice in heaven say: 'Now have come the salvation and the power and the kingdom of our God, and the authority of his Christ. For the accuser of our brothers, who accuses them before our God day and night, has been hurled down'" (Revelation 12:9, 10, NIV).

The next verse says, "And they overcame him by the blood of the Lamb." Not by the power of an outstretched hand with a club in it, but by the power of an outstretched hand with a spike through it. An outstretched hand with a towel in it. *A hand that washed dirty feet!*

You can read about that in John 13:1-5. It's an

amazing scene! The King of heaven and earth is kneeling before His disciples and washing their feet! We watch the almost unbelievable: Jesus takes the feet of Judas into His gentle hands—those hands so soon to be nailed to a cross because of Judas's betrayal—and tenderly washes them. Dear God! Is that not a tear in His eyes?

If I'd been God, I'd have taken that basin of water and poured it over Judas's scheming head! And while the other disciples looked on in amazement, I would have pointed wordlessly to the door, and he would have slunk out, water dripping from his treacherous locks.

But Jesus *was* God. And His tears mingled with the water He poured so lovingly over His betrayer's feet. He washed them with hands that, the prophet Isaiah says, have our names written on them! "Can a mother forget the baby at her breast and have no compassion on the child she has borne? Though she may forget, I will not forget you! See, I have engraved you on the palms of my hands" (Isaiah 49:15, 16, NIV).

Strange, isn't it, that the Bible so often stresses God's tender forbearance rather than His wrath. It's as if He wishes us to remember that the strength of the church does not reside in political power. The strength of the church resides in its avalanche of powerlessness, its tidal force of love. Love that will not let us go.

Better thank the Lord that I'm not God! Even I do!

## Chapter 3

# HERE COME DA JUDGE!

O n my first night on a Christian college campus, I found my way to the church for what they called vespers. After songs and prayer, a distinguished-appearing guest speaker, introduced as Dr. Stoehr, stepped to the pulpit. He opened his Bible, stood quietly as he pondered the words of Daniel 7:9, 10, and in a soft, German-accented voice began to read:

" 'I beheld till the thrones were cast down, and the Ancient of days did sit, whose garment was white as snow, and the hair of his head like the pure wool: his throne was like the fiery flame, and his wheels as burning fire. A fiery stream issued and came forth from before him: thousand thousands ministered unto him, and ten thousand times ten thousand stood before him: the judgment was set, and the books were opened.' "

I—who knew nothing of judgment—sat among the Christian "saints," petrified! So intense was the conviction that I would stand in judgment before God that as I write these words the same emotion seizes me. The meaning is sure: God has set a time when He will judge the world (Acts 17:31, RSV). However I might wish to escape it, I know that I shall stand one day before the judgment seat of Christ (Romans 14:10) to hear His verdict on what I've done—good or bad (2 Corinthians 5:10). I wondered whether the Judge was working His way through the alphabet. For the first time in my life, I wished my surname began with a Z—Zykoskee, Zinke, Zerububbal—anything further along than A–B–C–D–E–F–G–Hegstad. I knew that my name was not written in what Dr. Stoehr called the "Lamb's book of life." I sat. I shook. I could hear the crash of the Judge's gavel: "6 million years at 240 degrees"!

I've learned since that judgment can be good news. First, because it's fair. Second, because we can ensure a favorable verdict before we even enter the courtroom. Third, because both the defense attorney and the judge are on our side!

Still, a courtroom can be intimidating. A few months ago I was served a summons to testify in a case. I couldn't eat before going into the courtroom. While testifying, I had to deep-breathe to get my voice down from a panicky soprano. Nobody but nobody likes to go to court. Not even lawyers. You've got to pay them to get them in there!

We fear courts, even when we're in the right, for three reasons: first, we lack confidence in our legal system. It does not, after all, guarantee justice. And what if the jury finds you guilty?

Second, a study of sentencing in various states shows that sentences are hardly equitable. Blacks suffer longer than Whites for the same crime. Men get longer sentences than women. Homicides in Texas bring an average sentence of five and one-half years; in Illinois, 16 and one-half years. For statutory rape a man can get 10 years in New York, 50 years in California, 99 years in New Mexico, death in Delaware, and in Maine, a $500 fine! The average sentence for stealing a car in a nearby state is 41 months—four times longer than the average for forcible rape!

Finally, we fear judgment when it is fair. After all, we know what we deserve, and that's hardly a comforting thought. But hear me out.

## God's judgment is good news because it is fair.

"Fair" means, first of all, that God does not punish arbitrarily. In that courtroom above, the punishment will fit the crime. In fact, we write our own sentence on the very molecules of our mind. As one writer has observed: "By a life of rebellion, Satan and all who unite with him place themselves so out of harmony with God that His very presence is to them a consuming fire" (*The Desire of Ages,* p. 764; see Hebrews 12:29).

Earth is the testing ground between two eternities. Every person shall reap in judgment what is sown here. Here we come into harmony with God. Now is the time to groove channels into our minds through which the currents of heaven can flow unimpeded. Here we cooperate with God in rooting out every indulged vice. Here we learn to capture the celestial melody until, when the divine tuning fork is struck, our very being will resonate with the harmonies of heaven.

Punishment is not an arbitrary act on the part of God. It is the outworking of our own choices.

Further, a fair judgment means that all wrongs will be righted up there.

During World War II a German officer in Warsaw was ambushed by the Polish underground. In retaliation, 100 Poles were rounded up at random and taken to cells in the building called 25 Szucha Avenue. I recoiled when visiting it a few years ago. All about were terrible evidences of torture, pain, and death. Blood stained the walls and wooden floors. Ten at a time, the innocent captives were marched out and shot in retaliation for the officer's death. I read the last message of a young woman. She had traced it on the wall in lipstick:

"Nobody thinks of me and nobody knows
I am so alone girl 21 years of age and must
die guiltless
12. IX 43 Sunday ZR."

In every age the guiltless have died. The innocent have rotted in dungeons. God's people have been virtually wiped out in one age and corrupted in another. Truth has seemed "forever on the scaffold, wrong forever on the throne." And still millions go to bed at night, as Robert Louis Stevenson said, "with the half of a broken hope for a pillow."

But justice will come. Truth will triumph. John pictures the saints crying out "How long, O Lord, before you judge and avenge our blood on them that dwell on the earth?" (see Revelation 6:10). The answer, as the revelator makes clear, is just prior to the return of Jesus to reign. As a result of this judgment, all wrongs will be righted: "He that is unjust, let him be unjust still. . . . And, behold, I come quickly; and my reward is with me, to give every man according as his work shall be" (Revelation 22:12). The standard that divides the wicked and the righteous is a matter of record: "Blessed are they that do his commandments, that they may have right to the tree of life, and may enter through the gates into the city" (verse 14). The saints will be able to evaluate the records and confirm that everything a loving God could do was done on behalf of every person in that great cosmic courtroom. And the sinless beings on a million worlds will confirm that citizenship in the universal kingdom can be safely restored to the transformed inhabitants of Rebelworld.

Even the wicked, in the end—after they are raised in the second resurrection—kneel around the Holy City to acknowledge with all the rest of creation: "Great and marvelous are thy works, Lord God Almighty; just and true are thy ways" (Revelation 15:3). The consuming glory of God leaps forth, and soon the wicked are no more. Once again "one pulse of harmony and gladness beats throughout the vast creation. From Him who created all, flow life and light and gladness, throughout the realms of illimitable space. From the minutest atom to the greatest world, all things, animate and inanimate, in their unshaded beauty and perfect joy declare that God is love" (*The Great Controversy,* p. 678).

The poet asks:

> With His radiance splendid
> Will your light be blended,
> When His glory doth appear?

Yes, judgment is good news because it is fair. "Fair" means that God does not judge arbitrarily. He rights all wrongs on His way to making the whole universe one again!

### Judgment is good news because it enables us to clear our record before it is opened to the universe.

Timothy tells us that we can send our record of sins to court now and have it "fixed." (1 Timothy 5:24). With God's help we can ferret out every secret vice, even thoughts, that could, if uncorrected, leave us unprotected, without an advocate, in that final courtroom scene. It isn't a comfortable process; it feels like a dental drill inserted without novocaine into the spinal cord of conscience. I know.

Early in my experience as a Christian I lived next door to two female schoolteachers. They were young, attractive sun worshippers. Every time the sun came up, they came out—garbed in two towels each, strategically positioned and pinned. The towels were about the size of a Waldorf washcloth. Occasionally I'd put on my dark glasses and drop by to minister to their mortal souls. One day the Lord joined us in the backyard. (Being sun worshippers, they couldn't see or hear Him.) "Roland," He said, "out here in the desert the humidity isn't all that high. Why are your sunglasses all steamed up?"

"Why, it must be my fervor for their souls, Lord" (anything to get the Hound of heaven off the scent of sin).

"But," said the Lord, "I can't help noticing that their souls aren't where you're looking."

Says God's Word: "Some . . . sins are open beforehand, going before to judgment; and some . . . follow after" (1 Timothy 5:24). And those that follow after cannot be hidden—even behind dark sunglasses. But *they can be laid on Jesus beforehand.* God doesn't want us to carry lust into His courtroom. He wants us to turn it over to His Son, the Sin-bearer. "If we confess our sins, he is faithful and just to forgive us our sins, and to cleanse us from all unrighteousness" (1 John 1:9).

It didn't take me long to learn that the newborn Christian resembles a newborn baby. And newborn babies make a lot of mistakes—they fall down a lot until they learn to hold on to Mother's hand. They grab toys from each other; they sass Mother. Mothers know better than to expect perfection. So does our heavenly Father. As Paul wrote: "Stop evaluating Christians by what the world thinks about them or by what they seem to be like on the outside" (2 Corinthians 5:16, TLB). The Son of Son of God has already paid the penalty for all of our failures.

We've found that judgment can, indeed, be good news. First, because it is fair. Second, because we can cooperate with Christ in "fixing" our case before we enter the courtroom up there. And so we come to the third, and final, truth I've learned about judgment:

## Judgment is good news because both the defense attorney and the judge are on our side!

Yes, both our heavenly Father and His Son want to hand down a verdict in our favor! And from what I've shared with you of my troubled growth in Christ, you must know that's just the kind of advocate I need! I am a transgressor of God's holy law. I had broken it long before that Friday night vesper service. Long before I had even heard of judgment. Long before I met Jesus—and not a few times since. There's no way I can ever stand before God in that final judgment and plead "Not guilty!" By heaven's definition I'm a killer, for I have been angry with parents and enemies and friends alike. I'm an adulterer, because I have lusted; I'm a thief, because I have coveted. And further, Jesus has shown me that in some circumstances, at some time, I would have committed virtually every foul crime in the book. And so would you! If you don't believe that, you don't know yourself. And you don't know how far Jesus reached down to salvage you.

We should both be grateful, you and I, that Jesus is handling our case in court. He's sitting at the right hand of the Majesty on high (Hebrews 1:3). That's the place of power, the place of authority. The third chapter of the ancient prophecy of Zachariah describes the scene as the devil steps before the court and charges us with every foul deed we ever did—or even thought we'd like to do. When he finishes, the Father-Judge leans forward and asks Jesus, "Son, is that right? We can't have anyone like that up here!"

The Son goes over to the table holding the evidence and picks up a book. He begins to read. O Lord, can it be? Am I hearing right? Under my name is listed every good deed Jesus Christ did on earth! Most aren't even in the Bible, but there they are—under my name! And then He spells out what it meant when He paid our debt at Calvary. It offered:

• A sacrifice that completely covers confessed sins (Hebrews 10:12).

• New status with God—we're counted as free from sin, as if we had never entertained one bad thought! (verse 14).

• A new will with God's law inscribed so deeply on it that we won't ever forget it (verses 16, 17).

When Jesus finishes reading, the Father-Judge leans forward again and says, "Son, You got the right book?"

The Son picks it up again. It is titled the book of life. He holds it out to the Father in His nail-scarred hands and says, "Father, it's Your book."

And then I remember: "God was in Christ, restoring the world to himself, no longer counting [our] sins against [us], but blotting them out. . . . For God took the sinless Christ and poured into him our sins. Then, in exchange, He poured God's goodness into us" (2 Corinthians 5:19-21, TLB).

Now, I'm a person who likes bargains. This offer qualifies as extraordinary. So extraordinary and extravagant that it reminds me of a case. A case so exceptional that—well, decide for yourself.

Michael A. Musmanno, an associate justice of the Pennsylvania Supreme Court until shortly before his death, tells an astounding courtroom story in his autobiography, *Verdict*. As a young law student in 1925 he had visited a Paris courtroom. The defendant, Aida Valette, a young woman of 25, stood charged with hurling acid into the face of Jacqueline Claremont, her rival for the love of a young man, Charles Viviers.

Jacqueline, her face and neck hidden beneath wide bandages, sat at the witness bench. Only her eyes were visible, but they told much of suffering and of beauty. The golden strands of hair escaping from her fashionable turban, the graceful lines of her figure, the photograph of her prior to the assault—all spoke of surpassing loveliness.

From the witness stand Jacqueline told of the assault. "One day, just a year ago, while I walked along the street, I saw Aida approaching me. I caught a glimpse of a large openmouthed jar, and then I felt a million needles in my face. Where the acid struck my clothing, the garment parted as if it were paper before a flame. I could feel the skin on my face and neck dissolving." Convulsed with sobs, Jacqueline crumpled into her chair.

Jacqueline's doctor took the stand and described in harrowing detail the mordant impact of the acid, which, a year before, had reduced her face to a mask of spine-chilling grotesqueness.

Then it was that Aida Valette demanded the right to confront Charles Viviers, who had said in the courtroom that he still loved Jacqueline. Flanked by two gendarmes, she strode in front of him.

"Charles," she said in a surprisingly calm voice, "you have said that you will marry Jacqueline. But I know you do not love her. You only feel sorry for her. Once you see her hideous face you will hate yourself for your rash act. Witness now what you would have to look at every day of your life!"

Breaking loose from the guards, she lunged at Jacqueline, trying to rip the protecting bandages from her face. The public prosecutor restrained her just in time, and the guards shoved her, as she kicked and struggled, back into her chair.

The judge reprimanded her and announced a 20-minute recess.

When the court reconvened, counsel for the defense arose. "Mr. President," he said, addressing the judge, "my client is here charged with a grave offense—the crime of mayhem. I submit to the court that she has the right to demand that Mademoiselle Claremont's covering be removed so the jury can see for themselves whether the crime of mayhem has actually been established."

Over objections of the public prosecutor, the judge gave his ruling. Although regretting that Mademoiselle Claremont must be subjected to embarrassment, trial procedure compelled the granting of the defendant's request. "Until the wounds are revealed," said the judge, "all elements of the crime charged have not been proved legally."

"Mr. President!" Charles Viviers was on his feet. "Mademoiselle Claremont need not fear that her wounds will rob me of my devotion to her." Turning to the distraught girl, he said, "Jacqueline, I love you, and I will marry you today if you will have me. Let me remove the bandages and let us both stand before the world, unashamed and unafraid. I entreat you to let me do this."

"But Charles, you might not want me then . . . but do as you wish."

Speaking softly and reassuringly of his love, he tenderly touched the bandages. Not an eyelash flickered as he unwound the first strips, which, glistening in a shaft of sunlight, fell at the feet of the quivering girl. As the ribbon descended, a sneer curled Aida's lips. She would be found guilty, but in a moment she would have her revenge. As only two turns of the bandage remained, the judge spoke:

"Stop! Stop for a moment. I warn everyone in the courtroom, there will be no demonstration!"

Like a spiral of white, the last dressing floated to the floor. Only a square of gauze now hid Jacqueline's face. Tenderly Viviers lifted the corner of the protecting shield and pulled it away. As it fell from his fingers to the floor, the courtroom froze. Like a movie stopped on a frame, time seemed suspended. Then, with a cry of anguish, Jacqueline buried her face in her hands.

Gently, lovingly, Viviers lifted her to her feet and raised her head. Still no one spoke. Finally Jacqueline sobbed, "Give me a mirror. Let me see this Medusa's head that has transfixed you all."

A woman close by opened her purse and, as if in a trance, withdrew a small mirror, which she handed to the weeping girl. Slowly, Jacqueline lifted it, looked, gasped, and cried out, "NO!" For in the mirror she saw—perfection. Not a scar or blemish marred her beauty. "I don't understand," she stammered. "At the hospital I saw the pictures taken after I arrived, and I was so hideous that I haven't looked at my face since."

The public minister subpoenaed the girl's doctor, a plastic surgeon, and an hour later, after a recess, he took the stand. He explained that he had performed several operations on the girl but, fearing to raise hopes that might not be realized, had never told her of the extent of the skin grafts. "But now I am happy to say," he went on, "that the operations were successful, and I can assure all her friends that her beauty has been permanently restored."

Suddenly, spontaneously, the audience broke into

deafening applause, for in that moment the whole world had become beautiful again.

God grant that it may be thus with us when we stand before the judgment seat of Christ, our profile bandaged and hidden. When the enemy of our soul, he who had scarred us and defaced the image of God in us, demands that we be exposed to the gaze of the universe.

Then our Advocate will step forward and gently, lovingly, unwrap our bandages. And while the universe waits in breathless expectancy, we shall ask in agony of spirit, "Can He love me still?"

Oh, when the bandages fall away! Then shall we know the triumph of love, for from the universe assembled shall come the cry "His face, her face, is as the face of the dear Son!"

And from the Son shall we hear, "Well done, thou good and faithful servant. I won your case for you long ago. Because you accepted Me as your Savior and advocate, hear the good news: My grace is sufficient for you. Come on in!"

## Chapter 4

# AN
# OFFBEAT SUBJECT

It didn't take me long in a Bible class on the Old Testament to determine my favorite character. The book of Daniel rated high, not only because of its prophecies, but also because of the daring faith of the three Hebrew youth, with Daniel foremost. So forceful is the story of the handwriting on the wall that the phrase endures to our day, used in a somber context of crisis to come. For prophecy and for stories Daniel's book must rate first.

But for comfort, I most often turn to the book of Isaiah. I thrill to the assurance of chapter 49:1: "Before I was born the Lord called me; from my birth he has made mention of my name" (NIV). Mine, too!

Need assurance? "Can a mother forget the baby at her breast and have no compassion on the child she has borne? Though she may forget, I will not forget you! See, I have engraved you on the palms of my hands" (verses 15, 16, NIV). How parents must thrill to this assurance: "I will contend with those who contend with you, and I will save your children" (verse 25, RSV).

"Hear me, you who know what is right, you people who have my law in your hearts: Do not fear the reproach of men or be terrified by their insults" (Isaiah 51:7, NIV). "How beautiful on the mountains are the feet of those who bring good news, who proclaim peace, . . . who proclaim salvation, who say to Zion, 'Your God reigns!' " (Isaiah 52:7, NIV).

Want a special promise that you'll not be forgotten? " 'Though the mountains be shaken and the hills be removed, yet my unfailing love for you will not be shaken nor my covenant of peace be removed,' says the Lord, who has compassion on you" (Isaiah 54:10, NIV).

You've sampled just a taste of my favorite Old Testament character, Isaiah. And it is he to whom I'm indebted for asking (and answering) a question that has long troubled would-be Christians:

"Who among us shall dwell with the devouring fire? Who among us shall dwell with everlasting burnings?" (Isaiah 33:14, NKJV).

That question provokes anxiety in hearts. It did in mine. It made it difficult for me to love God: it raised the question of whether sinners are really going to suffer forever in the fires of hell. Isaiah's "everlasting burnings" sounds like the kind of hell that has turned many people away from the church. All the passages in Isaiah that reveal the abiding love of God for His children do not allay our anxiety over what He has to say about hell.

According to a recent poll, 60 percent of Americans believe there is a hell, in which those who have lived bad lives without regrets are eternally damned. A whopping 78 percent said they had a good to excellent chance of going to heaven, in which 72 percent professed belief. Those who professed no religion but believe in heaven or hell were the least optimistic, though only 9 percent anticipated an eternity in hell. One might conclude that hell is, indeed, a hot subject. So let's go—to the subject, that is!

**What are the fires of hell?** Certainly they are very real. They turn the earth into a lake of fire and brimstone (see Revelation 14:10). Says Peter: "The elements shall melt with fervent heat, the earth also and the works that are therein shall be burned up" (2 Peter 3:10).

Their effect on the wicked is terminal: They shall be as ashes under the feet of the righteous (see Malachi 4:3). "They shall be as though they had never been" (Obadiah 1:16, NEB).

Notice that these verses do not say that sinners burn forever, but rather that the *results* of hellfire are everlasting. Sinners receive everlasting *punishment,* not everlasting *punishing.* In Scripture "eternal" often refers to the result, not the process: note the expressions "eternal salvation" (Hebrew 5:9, NIV); "eternal judgment" (Hebrew 6:2, NIV); "eternal sin" (Mark 3:29, NIV); "eternal punishment" (Matthew 25:46, NIV); "eternal destruction" (2 Thessalonians 1:9, NRSV). It is not the process (the saving, the judging, the sinning, the punishing, the destroying) that is eternal, but the result (salvation, judgment, sin, punishment, destruction). It is a bit of a scandal that many Christian preachers and teachers have not yet figured this out, still advocating the discredited theory that God tortures His enemies forever! But according to Jude 7, Sodom and Gomorrah were burned with "eternal fire." Yet they are not still burning today. Second Peter 2:6 says that this fire reduced these cities to ashes, and that this is an example of what is going to happen to the wicked.

Surely, then, hell is very real, and we are not left in doubt about its terminal effects. But what *are* the fires of hell?

Isaiah asks, "Who among us shall dwell with the devouring fire?"—that is, with God! Says the writer of Hebrews, "Our God is a consuming fire" (Hebrews 12:29). That is, He is a consuming fire to the wicked:

"By a life of rebellion," one commentator concludes, "Satan and all who unite with him place themselves so out of harmony with God that His very presence is to them a consuming fire. The glory of Him who is love will destroy them" (*The Desire of Ages,* p. 764).

So it is the glory of God that destroys the wicked. Hell is to stand in the presence of God without the "fire insurance" He bought for us at Calvary.

**What made the glory of God destructive to some of His creation?** Not a change in the nature of God, who is the same "yesterday, and today, and forever" (Hebrews 13:8), but a change in the nature of His creation. Here is the story:

In the beginning there was harmony in heaven. All created beings sang the same songs and in the same key; everyone enjoyed perfect pitch.

But one day a new note was sounded by the choir director, Lucifer, later called Satan or the devil. "God is love" sang the choir; "God is selfish," whispered the director—though not very loud at first. It was a chilling note of dissonance and defiance, insinuating, insisting: "I would be like God! I will take the throne!"

God permitted Lucifer to sing his solo part until half the heavenly chorus was echoing the offbeat refrain. This was the first revolt against harmony. God did not immediately put Lucifer's program off the air, for the angels could not then foresee the note on which his composition must inevitably end. Had Lucifer been summarily blotted out of existence, some of God's sons and daughters would have served Him from fear rather than from love. Lucifer's own offbeat notes must condemn him.

Until the rebellious solo, the angels had scarcely thought of there being a divine tuning fork—an instrument of law—to which they must tune their lives. They knew only that while the allegiance of love was their theme, perfect harmony sounded throughout God's universe. When the Creator, God's Son, sang a solo lead and the score called for an answering chord, it was their delight to render it. But now, confused by Lucifer's accusations, charmed by the subtlety of his refrain, nearly half the angels left the heavenly choir and formed their own troop. Lucifer's rebellious note was destined to change the tenor of the universe, for it found lodging in the hearts of other angels. As a pebble dropped in water causes ripples to spread in ever-widening circles, so the accusation of Lucifer impacted the whole creation.

The Father called a meeting of the inhabitants of heaven. Boldly Lucifer set forth his claims; unblushingly he made known his dissatisfaction that Christ should be preferred before him. He argued that he should be taken into the inner councils of the Godhead and be permitted to help write the score of the creation oratorio for Earth and its inhabitants, which God's Son was to create. The Father informed Lucifer that in His Son, and in Him alone, was invested creative power. He told him that heavenly beings were required to harmonize with the divine tuning fork—His holy law.

Sneeringly Lucifer expressed his contempt for authority. Law was a restriction on liberty, and must be abolished. All should be free to find their own pitch. Says the Sacred Record: "And there was war in heaven: Michael and his angels fought against the dragon; and the dragon fought and his angels, and prevailed not; neither was their place found any more in heaven" (Revelation 12:7, 8). The words convey the vibrations of cosmic conflict—the lightning of slashing lasers, the agony of splitting atoms, as Lucifer, the light bearer, he who had given the pitch to the angelic choir, is driven from heaven, and his angels with him.

It may have been God's plan to create a new world, which we know as Earth, and populate it with a new creation that sparked Lucifer's revolt. For the details we'll have to wait for the return of God's Son to our sin-battered world. Until then, enjoy a few moments of the Creation oratorio, sung by the loyal angels against a backdrop of the starry heavens. Encompassing seven movements, it started with a note of nothingness on a background of indigo. Suddenly the Creator struck a majestic chord, and light was, and earth and water. Before the awestruck audience of the universe, the great Creation oratorio moved toward its climax. "And God said, Let us make man in our image. . . . In the image of God created he him; male and female created he them" (Genesis 1:26, 27). And the morning stars shouted for joy, and the heavens thundered their applause.

Then came a new note: the sound of lions and lambs frolicking together; of birds flittering from tree to tree, their mellow-toned music echoing with sweet accord to the pizzicato of breeze in glen and forest. And the voices of the holy pair united with the rest of the creation in harmonious songs of love and praise for the Father and His dear Son. "And God saw everything that he had made, and, behold, it was very good" (verse 31).

Meanwhile, Lucifer, exiled from heaven, stood amazed at his condition. His happiness was gone. The countenances of the angels cast out with him were gloomy and despairing. Instead of strains of sweetest music, discord and disharmony filled the ear of the great rebel leader. Not a quartet, no, not so much as a duet, could be sung without sour notes of jealousy and suspicion creeping into the score. Is it not all a horrible dream? Is he forever shut out of heaven?

*Humanity!* If he could cause these new creatures

to rebel, would God not find a way to reinstate them? And if so, then why not him and his followers? Human beings must be made to rebel!

God created Adam and Eve, not as limited automatons, but as advanced creatures with the power of reason and the possibility of rebellion. They were free to exercise their choice, for only from free voices can come melody to delight the heart of the Father of all. However, God had warned them of Lucifer's rebellion. One tree was denied them as a test of allegiance—the tree of the knowledge of good and evil. How bitter its fruits!

Earth's parents succumbed to Lucifer's seductive refrain. The prince of darkness becomes the prince of the new world. The glory of God that encircled His children in garments of light departs; the music of their souls is silenced. Now is heard only the voice of lament and recrimination: "The serpent beguiled me, and I did eat." We phrase it a bit differently today: "The devil made me do it." And still we hear the echo of rebellion: "All must be free to do their own thing. To sound their own pitch. To write their own score." Millennia removed, we yet hurl our rebellious notes against the rafters of eternity.

The guilty pair were driven from Eden—so they could not continue to eat of the tree of life and immortalize sin. As Adam looked on the first dying leaf, the sorrow of his soul was as that of parents today over the death of a firstborn. Decay without was matched by decay within; subtly the very molecules of their being moved into new orbits; their pattern of thinking changed; the woof of righteousness became the warp of sin.

The glory of God that gave light and life to His creation now brings pain. Not because the nature of the light has changed, but because humanity no longer vibrates on the same plane. The open communion Adam and Eve had enjoyed with their Creator is no longer possible. Indeed, humanity exists at all only because One has pledged Himself to die for the fallen race, and is counted the Lamb "slain from the foundation of the world."

Sacred history becomes a record of God seeking His fallen children, and betimes meeting with them; but no more face to face. Not now can they behold the glory of God and live (Exodus 33:20). *Hell is to stand in the presence of God without a shield of righteousness. To lives out of harmony with the tuning fork of heaven, God's very presence is a consuming fire.* "For the Lord your God is a consuming fire" (Deuteronomy 4:24, NKJV; see also Hebrews 12:29). "The Lord your God is the one who goes across ahead of you like a devouring fire" (Deuteronomy 9:3, NIV).

Now to our third question:

**What will bring hell to an end?** Obviously not a change in the nature of God, the same yesterday, and today, and forever. It should be obvious that hell ends after it has achieved its purpose of eternal destruction of sin and sinners. But that's not the whole truth.

To understand the end, we need to understand the beginning. Inscribed on the seed is the story of its harvest. The beginning of hell, as we have seen, was Lucifer and the strange malignancy called sin, which was born in his heart. The beginning of hell was his ambition to be like God, to mount His throne. The beginning of hell was his accusation against the character of God and his attack on God's holy law.

In order for harmony to be restored, for the entire universe to beat again with one pulse of gladness, everyone involved in the conflict must be satisfied that the claims of Satan are baseless; that sin has demonstrated its self-destructive nature; that the allegiance of love is the only basis for eternal happiness. The character and aims of God must be exonerated; divine love and justice must be demonstrated; sin must be exterminated. Only then can hell have its end.

Satan and his fellow angels had sinned in the presence of great light. Sin was born in them. Scripture plainly teaches that hell was prepared "for the devil and his angels" (Matthew 25:41), and that it will eventually reduce Satan to ashes:

"You were anointed as a guardian cherub, for so I ordained you. You were on the holy mount of God; you walked among the fiery stones. You were blameless in your ways from the day you were created till wickedness was found in you. . . . So I drove you in disgrace from the mount of God, and I expelled you, O guardian cherub, from among the fiery stones. Your heart became proud on account of your beauty, and you corrupted your wisdom because of your splendor. So I threw you to the earth; I made a spectacle of you. . . . So I made a fire come out from you, and it consumed you, and I reduced you to ashes on the ground in the sight of all who were watching" (Ezekiel 28:14-18, NIV).

Because Satan's immediate destruction would not have left the dimensions of sin clearly defined, he was to be permitted to live long enough for the fallacies of his rival government to be demonstrated. The citizens of his kingdom must be given opportunity to bear witness for or against his claims. Their falseness clearly demonstrated, he could be destroyed, for the universe, once convinced of God's wisdom and love, would not again trifle with sin. But with humanity, a new element was introduced into the sin equation. For their disobedience Adam and Eve deserved death. But their sin was not so great as that of Lucifer, who revolted in the presence of God Himself. Nevertheless, divine justice demanded their death, for they had transgressed the constitution of the universe. Yet divine love desired that they live—they who were the crowning act of God's creation, made in the image of God, and heirs to a glorious destiny. Two words summarize God's solution. First:

**Bethlehem.** The Lord of heaven comes to pitch His tent beside the tents of humanity. He comes not with the glory He had with the Father before the world was made, but as a baby, clothed in the veil of flesh, with no special beauty.

Oh, what love! He who is the express image of the Father tabernacles with humanity—becomes eternally one of the human race. Again, through the veil of flesh, the character of God, the very life of God, "flowed out in currents of sympathy and tenderness. The aged, the sorrowing, and the sin-burdened, the children at play in their innocent joy, the little creatures of the groves, the patient beasts of burden—all were happier for His presence. He whose word of power upheld the worlds would stoop to relieve a wounded bird. There was nothing beneath His notice, nothing to which He disdained to minister" (*The Desire of Ages,* p. 74).

Can we grasp what happened? Divinity is veiled with humanity so that fallen humanity can look on God and live! In the life of Christ is seen the express image of the Father, and Satan's accusations against Him are shown to be lies.

The second part of God's solution can likewise be summed up in one word:

**Calvary.** Could it be that we have been given a cosmic science, a cosmic vocabulary, to help us better understand cosmic events—to better understand Calvary?

In May 1946 a young scientist was carrying out a

daring experiment at Los Alamos, the U.S. atomic test center. To determine the amount of U-235 necessary to sustain a chain reaction, he would push two hemispheres of uranium together. Just as the mass became critical, he would separate the spheres with his screwdriver, thus stopping the chain reaction. But one day the screwdriver slipped. The hemispheres of uranium came too close together. Instantly the room was filled with a dazzling bluish haze. Young Louis Slotin, instead of ducking and protecting himself, tore the two hemispheres apart with his hands, stopping the chain reaction. By this, he saved the others in the room. He told a companion, "You'll come through all right, but I haven't the faintest chance." Nine days later he died in agony.

Twenty centuries ago the Son of God walked into sin's most concentrated radiation. He came when the hemispheres of sin had reached critical mass. When the countdown of the centuries reached its end, He who made the atom allowed wicked men to trigger the cruel device we call Calvary. To interrupt the chain reaction of sin, to stop its deadly radiation, He gave His life at ground zero.

The deadly fallout of sin had written death on every nerve, every tissue, every cell of our bodies. "Death passed upon all" (Romans 5:12). Sin had built up in intensity until it became a critical mass at Calvary. But the Son of God threw His body across the fury of its chain reaction and broke its power! His hands will bear the mark of this encounter throughout eternity!

Calvary—there for all who believe is the answer to hell. There, on the testing grounds of the universe, there at ground zero, a voice from the command center of the universe counted backward—5, 4, 3, 2, 1—and two spheres were thrust together. One of purified love, one of petrified hate—and the cataclysmic consequence reverberated from star to star. The price for sin was paid. When Jesus rose from the grave, death was conquered and hope was reborn for lost sinners. "For God so loved the world, that he gave his only begotten Son, that whosoever believeth in him should not perish, but have everlasting life" (John 3:16). At Calvary God wrote a fire insurance policy and signed it with blood.

Until Calvary a few in the universe were yet confused by Satan's claims. But there, at ground zero, the testing grounds of the universe, the destructive power of even an atom of sin was demonstrated. There the benevolent and eternal nature of the law of God was settled. It was shown to be a law of love. It was shown to be central to the happiness of all created beings. There the Son of God paid the penalty for all our sins! When I remember that Calvary is but a faint revelation to our sin-dimmed senses of the agony that has been in the heart of God from the inception of sin, I can but stand silent, awed, before this revelation of His love.

Bethlehem. Calvary. God's answer to hell. Thus we are "reconciled to God by the death of his Son," and so we "shall be saved by his life" (Romans 5:10).

We come to my last question:

**Who, then, shall dwell with the devouring fire?** Says the prophet Isaiah: "You can survive if you say and do what is right. Don't use your power to cheat the poor and don't accept bribes. Don't join with those who plan to commit murder or to do other evil things" (Isaiah 33:15, TEV). The prophet emphasizes that people reap what they sow. Mark it on your heart: God's judgments are not arbitrary. *Every person determines the length of his or her own sentence! Great sins resist the consuming fire the longest; lesser sins lead to a shorter time in the consuming fire.*

Earth is the testing ground between two eternities. Here we must come into harmony with God. Here we must groove channels in our minds through which the currents of heaven can flow unimpeded. Here we must root out every trace of sin until, when the divine tuning fork is struck, the very molecules of our being will vibrate in harmony with it.

A wrong understanding of hell kept me from loving God. The right concept won my heart and allegiance. I hope it will win yours.

## Chapter 5

# BEYOND ROPE'S END

I can see Seeker now, as a Japanese film portrays him: A lonely figure walking out of a city into the vast wilderness of the desert. He is searching, he says, for a new kind of life, for a creature that will bear his name and make him in some sense immortal. All day Seeker moves across the shifting sands, his need unmet. At night a stranger comes and guides him into a deep pit. At its bottom is a house. "You may spend the night here," says the stranger.

Seeker descends a 100-foot rope ladder into the pit. Within the house is a woman who feeds him and shows him a place to sleep. In the morning he finds the rope ladder is gone. He is trapped. Angrily he turns on the woman. "Time is important to me," he snaps, and charges up the sand walls. They collapse on him. When food is let down on a rope, he seeks to climb out. It is released by unseen hands.

Then, horrified, he sees a river of sand, driven by the wind, pouring endlessly over the rim. The woman explains that every night she must shovel the sand out of the pit and send it up in buckets on the rope. If no sand goes up, no food comes down.

"Don't you feel that all this is meaningless," he asks, "moving sand to live, living to move sand?"

One dark night, with the help of a rope he has woven, he escapes. "Free!" "Free!" he shouts, racing aimlessly among the dunes. Suddenly he falls into quicksand. When he cries for help, he is rescued and returned to the pit. Slowly he loses hope.

And then, in the bottom of a barrel sunk into the sand, he finds cool, clear water. He is amazed. What miracle is this that draws water from sand, coolness from blazing waste? He ponders the meaning. In the desert he has found water. In his fate, has he discovered the meaning of his life? He contemplates the reflection of his face. Is this the creature he has come seeking? Or is meaning beyond rope's end?

He looks up. The ladder is in place. He is free to go. Will he? Should he?

The film is a modern parable. The man and woman are every man and every woman. Their hellhole is Prison Earth; their dilemma that of all humanity; their questions those that have obsessed humanity throughout history. What is the meaning of our existence? Are we the result of the chance collision of molecules in a random universe? Is there no escape from our appalling predicament? And if there is, does it lie beyond rope's end? Is there, anywhere in the universe, someone worthy of our worship?

The questions, I submit, are crucial to our happiness. For the man and woman in the parable—you and me—have been given an urgent message: "Fear God and give glory to Him, for the hour of His judgment has come; and worship Him who made heaven and earth, the sea, and springs of water" (Revelation 14:7, NKJV).

Notice that worship is central in the last great confrontation between good and evil. The Bible indicates that humanity's fate is somehow involved in the answer to the question "Whom should we worship?"

In the parable, the answer is to be found in the desert.

Let's examine the metaphors of this modern parable: the seeker, the pit, the rope ladder, and the clear water in the burning sand.

### The Seeker

Seeker is the secular person who (1) rejects every form of religious faith and worship; or (2) simply dismisses faith and worship as irrelevant in this modern world; or (3) while professing faith and worship, renders them irrelevant by his or her indifference.

Secular humanity wears many masks.

**1. The mask of scientism.** This is worn by those who have come to believe that even questions of origin, nature, and destiny find definitive answers not in God's Word but in science. You'll find such closet secularists even in churches. Even behind pulpits.

**2. The mask of materialism.** Communism, you'll recall, was based on dialectical materialism. Capitalism's motivation most often is materialism. In our country its sacred writings are *Forbes, Money* magazine, and the *Wall Street Journal*.

The materialist's security does not reside in such a text as "Consider the lilies of the field, how they grow," but in Prudential's "Own a piece of the rock." Not in "Fear not, little flock; for it is your father's good pleasure to give you the kingdom," but in "Fear not, Oh ye of little savings; your Social Security check is in the mail."

**3. The mask of humanism.** This mask is worn by the person who sees the image of self and concludes that he or she is the answer to humanity's dilemma. The humanist seeks to reduce Jesus to a humanitarian who asks only that we be religious. The real Jesus asks much more of us than the humanistic Jesus; He asks us to be like Him—to be re-created in

His image. For He knows that the "one dark blot on the sunshine of our days" is, as Carlyle said, "the shadow of self." It is secular humanity that seeks vainly for meaning in the shifting sands of life. It is even secular humanity that has precipitated the emergence of a militant religious fundamentalism.

*Humanist* magazine, the mouthpiece of the American Humanist Association, observed: "The basis for mankind's future must be waged and won in the public school classrooms by teachers who correctly perceive their role as the proselytizer of a new faith; a religion of humanism . . . utilizing a classroom instead of a pulpit to convey humanist values in whatever subject they teach."

## The Pit

We left secular humanity trapped in a pit, moving sand to live, living to move sand. We know the feeling: Business reversals. Debts piling up. Inflation eating the heart out of savings. A marriage going nowhere. Shoveling sand to live, living to shovel sand.

Secular humanity escapes the shifting sands by its own effort, only to fall into quicksand—the ultimate metaphor that reminds us of Jesus' saying that you cannot build an enduring house of faith on shifting sand.

A few years ago a cabinet official talked to a select group of American student leaders at the White House. He told them, basically, to be good—good citizens, good people. When he finished, a Harvard University student asked respectfully, "Sir, can you tell us on what your moral values are founded?"

The official stood silent for what seemed an eternity before the expectant youth. Then, soft-voiced, he replied: "I'm sorry; I do not know."

Speaking of secular humanity's moral dilemma, the late philosopher David Klein observed:

"The experience of learning that an entire civilization is founded on nothing solid morally; that it is shot through and through with hypocrisy; that [there is] nothing in it to give life meaning—this has been so overwhelming a shock that it has left [the secular human being] largely mute, inarticulate, confused, unable to cope. He can literally be sure of nothing."

A worldwide moral declension does not happen overnight. Apostasy is not announced by trumpets. As *America* magazine put it: small changes "take place imperceptibly, in thousands of tiny, almost unnoticed ways, through infinitesimal shifts of emphasis—now here, now there, until the thing is done. Then, and only then, we who have lived unconsciously through the process reach the stage where suddenly, as though empowered to recognize it for the first time, we can perceive the difference the years have made."

Yes, we're down in the pit—that hellhole called Planet Earth—cut off from forgotten friends in distant stars, alienated from that Friend who came down to reacquaint us with the transcendent. And we pray, "Even so come, Lord Jesus—but please, Lord, not before we've had a few more years of the good life down here."

There are yet two unexplored metaphors in our modern parable: the rope ladder and the water in the midst of the burning sand. (If the story line seems a bit grim to this point, I've sneaked a look at the ending, and there's good news: everything comes out all right.)

## The Rope Ladder

One night in the desert between Beersheba and Haran a lonely man lay down to sleep. He took a stone and used it for his pillow. A fugitive from his country, marked for death by a vengeful brother, he had searched in vain for a way out of his self-made pit. As he slept, "he had a dream in which he saw a stairway resting on the earth, with its top reaching to heaven, and the angels of God were ascending and descending on it. There above it stood the Lord, and he said: 'I am the Lord. . . . I am with you and will watch over you wherever you go, and I will bring you back to this land. I will not leave you until I have done what I have promised you.' When Jacob awoke from his sleep, he thought, 'Surely the Lord is in this place, and I was not aware of it'" (Genesis 28:12-16, NIV).

Yes, God Himself came down to visit His creation. Two thousand years ago He came down to the pit to become forever one of us. He too went into the desert to pray for creatures who would bear His name. He is the rope. The living rope. And even among those who wear the mask called atheist, there are some who, confronted with today's dilemmas, are reaching out for Him.

## The Water

Cool, clear water in the midst of burning sand. What miracle is this that draws water from sand! Seeker bends and contemplates the reflection of his face. Is this the creature he has come seeking?

As he looks, the centuries dissolve and flow: the barrel becomes a well at the entrance to the valley of Shechem in ancient Samaria. By it a Stranger rests. At noon a woman of Samaria approaches. "Will you give me a drink?" He pleads.

She is puzzled. "You are a Jew and I am a [despised] Samaritan woman. How can you ask me for a drink?" (For Jews do not associate with Samaritans.)

"Jesus answered her, 'If you knew the gift of God and who it is that asks you for a drink, you would have asked him and he would have given you living water. . . . Whoever drinks the water I give him will never thirst. Indeed, the water I give him will become in him a spring of water welling up to eternal life'" (John 4:7-14, NIV).

Other wells go dry; every human resolve fails; riches, honors—all will be lost. But the water of life never fails.

This ancient story answers questions about our existence and our predicament that have obsessed all humanity. It tells us that the being Seeker viewed in the water is not the answer to our quest for meaning or deliverance. In Jesus' phrase "living water," and in His insistence that the true seeker must worship the Father in spirit and in truth, Jesus repeats His instruction to Nicodemus: "You must be born again."

Salvation does not reside in self. Humanism can leave us only as it left Aldous Huxley—"born wandering between two worlds, one dead and the other powerless to be born, and [having] made in a curious way the worst of both." Seeker must climb the ladder and go—go to his spouse with the good news of salvation. Go to their children. Go to their neighbors. Go to the Seekers of the world, reaching across walls of exclusiveness. For every true disciple is born into the kingdom of God with a mission—to spread the good news of salvation.

The disciples of Jesus thought that loyalty to their own nation and their own "church" required them to build a Berlin Wall between themselves and the Samaritans. They were bigoted. At that well Jesus taught them that true disciples don't build walls. They tear them down!

And now we come to the crux of Seeker's quest: Whom shall we worship, and where? The woman of Samaria, her conscience sparked into tingling awareness of guilt by the Stranger's revelation of her lifestyle, tries a theological diversion (don't we all, at such a time!): Gesturing toward Mount Gerizim, she says to Jesus: "Our fathers worshiped on this mountain; and you say that in Jerusalem is the place where men ought to worship" (John 4:20, RSV).

The worship at Mount Gerizim was tinctured with idolatry. No wonder, then, that Jesus pointed her to worship at Jerusalem. But even Jerusalem would not be forever the place of true worship. Said Jesus, "The hour is coming when you shall worship the Father neither at Gerizim nor in Jerusalem" (see verse 21).

Jerusalem had built a king-sized wall of partition between God's chosen people and "outsiders." Jerusalem stood for bigotry. Where, then, should one worship? Jesus answered, in effect, "Neither in a place of apostasy nor a place of bigotry. In fact, you don't need to go to a mountain to worship. You can worship in the desert. You can worship in your closet. You can worship at your work. But don't forget to meet in My house—and make it even more an imperative as the day of My return approaches" (see John 4:1-43 and Hebrews 10:25).

Now we are ready to put all the answers together and to understand what is at stake in the secular quest. At the beginning of His ministry Jesus went into the desert to pray for creatures who would bear His name. And one from the depths of hell came to offer Him all the kingdoms of the world for the sale price of a bended knee. "All this I will give you," said the prince of darkness, "if you will bow down and worship me" (Matthew 4:9, NIV).

And Jesus answered, "Away from me, Satan! For it is written: 'Worship the Lord your God, and serve him only'" (verse 10, NIV). The devil left Him—not to lick his wounds, but rather to plot his strategy to get from the church the worship he could not get from its Founder. Has he been successful? Ask the millions who themselves, while professing to worship God, are asking What is right? What is wrong? What is true? What is false? The hundreds of denominations in America can't all be right. Ask your neighbor to recite the first commandment. Or the fourth. Christians do not agree even on which day is the Sabbath! Most will admit that they worship on the first day of the week, contrary to the commandment to worship on the seventh day. Why?

Ironically, only the fourth of the Ten Commandments reveals both who is to be worshipped and how.

The Jesus of the desert says, "Thou shalt worship the Lord thy God, and him only shalt thou serve" (Matthew 4:10). The Jesus of Revelation says, "Worship him that made heaven, and earth, and the sea, and the fountains of waters" (Revelation 14:7). That's our assignment as we live to give God glory.

Once before, in a showdown between pagan forces and followers of God on Mount Carmel, two opinions prevailed about worship. Two altars were built. Two sacrifices offered. But the God who made heaven and earth and the sea and the fountains of waters let His fire fall on only one.

In Revelation 13 Jesus points to a second Mount Carmel. Fire is to fall again at end time: a firefall of counterfeit wonders and miracles, by which all nations shall be deceived (Revelation 18:23). As a result, the world shall turn on those who keep the commandments of God and bear testimony to Jesus Christ. Truth matters. Ultimately, it will be a life-or-death affair.

And so out of the parable of the seeker, the ladder, and the cool water in the burning sand hope is born—hope that Someone out there knows us, loves us, and someday soon will come to rescue us from this hellhole and introduce us to the family of God out there in the great beyond.

Of course, that is not the secularist's hope.

In the summer of 1977 a NASA space vehicle, *Voyager II,* looked back over its shoulder and took a last picture of Planet Earth. Beyond *Voyager's* camera the planets spread against the blackness of space like jewels on velvet. Saturn and Jupiter were to the right of the sun. To the left, the small red point of light was Mars. Venus appeared to be yellow. And between them, Earth signaled its presence as a blue point of light. That's us. That's home—a lonely blue dot almost lost against the background spangle and glory of the billions of stars in the Milky Way.

*Voyager's* creators hope that sometime, in the next billions of years, somewhere among the stars, beings alien to us will find *Voyager* and decipher its message. On it is a golden jacket containing information from the pit of our estrangement, our aloneness. *Voyager* carries greetings in 55 human languages and one whale language; a 12-minute sound essay, including a kiss, a baby's cry, and an EEG record of the meditations of a young woman in love; 115 pictures, digitally encoded, on our science, our civilization, and ourselves; and 90 minutes of Earth's greatest hits—Eastern and Western, classical and folk, including a Navajo night chant, an African girls' initiation song, a Peruvian wedding song, a Japanese shakuhachi piece, Bach, Beethoven, Mozart, Stravinsky, Louis Armstrong, and Chuck Berry singing "Johnny B. Goode."

*Voyager's* creators were hoping that Someone is out there, watching, as the song says, from a distance. But God is much nearer at hand than that. Our prayer can reach Him here and now:

O God!
You who never can err, for You are the Way;
You whose infinite kingdom is flooded with day;

You whose eyes behold all, for You are the Light,
Look down on us gently who journey by night.

For the pity revealed in Your loneliest hour,
Forsaken, self-bound, and self-emptied of power;
You who, even in death, had all heaven in sight,
Look down on us gently who journey by night.

On the road to Emmaus, they thought You were
    dead,
Yet they saw You and knew in the breaking of
    bread,
Though the day was far spent, in Your face there
    was light.
Look down on us gently who journey by night.

## Chapter 6

# IS GOD LOOKING GOOD?

God's not getting the best publicity these days. A lot of people seem to be holding Him responsible for a lot of problems—disasters, suffering, injustice, deaths. Here are a few samples:

• Three unattended children burned to death in a Washington, D.C., suburb while their mother was on an errand next door. They were: Joseph and Jason, 3-year-old twins, and their 18-month-old brother, Philip. Sobbed the mother: "Why did it have to happen to me? I was gone only a few minutes. There is no God! If there were, He wouldn't have let this happen to me!"

• In Miami, Florida, Hugh McNatt, 42, an electrician, joined a Baptist church. He began to tithe after the pastor promised blessings and reward. In a handwritten suit filed in Dade County court, McNatt asked for a return of $800. He says he didn't receive the benefits promised.

• When a telephone pole fell on his car during a storm, Rodney Bowman, of Florin, Pennsylvania, suffered a broken back. He sued the Columbia Telephone Company for $10,830 in damages. In defense, the company argued that the incident was "an act of God," a charge heard in courts since 1581.

• A child wrote to "Dear Abby," "My Sunday school teacher says that God is everywhere. Please put this letter in the paper and maybe He will see it.

"Dear God: Why did You let my brother die? When he was hit by the car, my mother prayed to You to let him live, but You wouldn't. My little brother was only 2 years old, and he couldn't have sinned so bad that You had to punish him that way. Everyone says You are good and can do anything You want to do. You could have saved my little brother, but You let him die. You broke my mother's heart. How can I love You?"

• Ted Turner, billionaire founder of CNN, was raised in a Catholic–Episcopal home. He had planned to be a missionary. He was a believer until, when he was 20, his teenage sister died of a rare form of lupus. For five years, Turner says, "I prayed 30 minutes every day for God to save her, and He didn't. A kind and loving God wouldn't let my sister suffer so much." At last he told God, "I don't want to have anything to do with You."

Dostoyevsky's Ivan Karamazov observed that if "God's truth demands the tortured cry of a single innocent child, then God's truth is not worth the price of admission."

Tens of thousands of children died in the gas ovens of Auschwitz, Dachau, Buchenwald, and Triblinka. They were part of the 6 million killed, 6 million of those God called His "chosen people." (Small wonder that some say, "I hope He doesn't choose me"!)

In Verdi's opera *Othello* the baritone, Iago, sings the following impious aria: "I believe in a cruel God who has created me in His own image, and I worship Him in hatred."

Tens of millions today don't worship Him at all. They call themselves "dialectical materialists" and charge that religion is the opiate of the masses. I once saw their exhibits of God's handiwork in the antireligious museum in Leningrad. Before the fall of Communism I walked through it, along with hundreds of schoolchildren who were being introduced to God. In one section we saw a Madonna with tear-streaked plaster cheeks. The guide showed us the rubber bulb the priest had squeezed to bring tears as he begged for rubles to stop her crying.

"God is a fraud," said the guide.

In another section we saw reconstructions of Christians torturing fellow Christians to bring them into the "loving" embrace of God. Said the Leningrad guide, "God is cruel."

In still another section we were shown pictures from the early 1930s, when tens of millions of Soviets starved to death. Said the guide: "The church had tens of millions of rubles worth of gold and silver." I got the message: God doesn't care about human misery and need. I took pictures of the wide-eyed children who marveled at the inhumanity of human beings to other human beings and the uncaring God they serve—all this in the name of God!

Soon after my baptism I began to study theology to determine more fully what God is really like. I read what the theologians had to say—Barth, Brunner, Tillich, Kierkegaard. And I gave my convoluted, compounded, footnoted, annotated definitions of God, the omnipotent one, the omniscient one, the omnipresent one—the one utterly utter, the ultimate ground of being. (No, I didn't understand what it all meant, any better than you do!)

Today I've got my theology down to five words: God's got to look good. A whole theology in five words! Some time ago I baptized John, and told him, "Your mission is to make God look good!" I've expanded the details of that mission a bit in the intervening years. Let me share a few thoughts with you.

God's got to look good, first, in the way He deals with His creation. Consider the way He dealt with Lucifer, the rebellious angel who introduced sin into God's universe. God could have put out His finger and squashed him. Or He could have sentenced him to a concentration camp in some dark corner of the universe and left him there to rot forever. But instead He permitted him to spread his dissatisfaction to Planet Earth as a proving ground so that we might experience the struggle and make our own decision about God's law, justice, and grace in dealing with transgressors. We can believe that God did all that love can do to draw Lucifer back. We can believe this because of what He did for us when we sinned. He decided that humanity was worth saving—even at the cost called Calvary. There was risk involved in Christ's mission to this world, as there was in the Creation. In the most fantastic event of the ages, God Himself came down and became one of us, forever. He was the Word, the Communicator, of what God really is like.

And what did He have to say to erring earthlings? Let's examine one encounter. An adulteress was brought to Him one day by those who had caught her in the act. Her accusers wanted her stoned, as the law provided. Jesus responded that the one without sin among them could hurl the first stone. You wouldn't believe what happened next, if you hadn't read the story! Jesus knelt and began writing something in the sand. And maybe His handwriting was just enough like a doctor's to make every onlooker believe he was reading a diagnosis of his own sins there. At any rate, they all slunk away, and Jesus and the woman were alone.

What a chance to canker her conscience with guilt! And then to put her on probation, with orders to report on her activities once a month. What did this God-man do? Jesus says to her, "Where are your accusers? Hasn't anyone condemned you?" She looks around. "No, no one, Lord." And He says, "Neither do I condemn you. Go and sin no more."

Kind of makes you want to continue the conversation with a God like that, doesn't it?

"But Lord," you say, "think of all the bad things I've done."

And He would reply: "I'd rather not. Instead, let's think of all the good things I've done. You see, when you accept Me as your Savior, My sinless record is credited to your account."

"But I'll slip, Lord. I'm a wicked person."

"Your dependence is not on your weakness, but on My strength—on what I can do for you, not on what you can't do for yourself. And even if you slip, you'll be treated as though you were righteous, so long as you cling to Me!"

"But Lord, what about my feelings and urges? Will You charge them against me?"

"No, I'm setting you free from guilt and fear of them."

"But what will God think of me if . . ."

"You're not to be anxious about what My Father thinks of you, but what He thinks of Me, His Son, your Savior. When He accepts Me, He accepts you. It's as simple as that. For He, that one who knew no sin, has made Me to be sin for you, so that you might once again become His child" (see 2 Corinthians 5:21).

If you'd like to continue this conversation at your leisure, you can construct it from Romans 4 through 8, as I did.

We can happily conclude that in His relationship with sinners, God looks great! But there's still the problem of human suffering, isn't there? And children writing to God to say, "You killed my little brother. You broke my mother's heart. How can I love You?"

Is God really the great heartbreaker?

Satan, God's conniving adversary, once came before the security council of the universe. The story is told in what may be the oldest book in the Bible: Job. God asked Satan whether he had noticed the faithfulness of Job, a man who appeared to truly love God. In response, Satan charged that Job would curse God if He laid His hand on him! The Lord corrected the record—it is, after all, Satan's hand, not God's, that brings torment upon humanity. God had such faith in Job that He permitted Satan to have his way with him—within limits. It was Satan, then, who (let me contemporize the account) put sugar in the tanks of Job's limos, reduced his 100,000 shares of IBM to worthless paper, slaughtered his family, and afflicted Job with herpes. What a test!

What if Mr. Job had decided to hang it up? He had no way of knowing that the theater of the universe was filled—standing room only—with majestic beings watching his performance. The review being written would thrill audiences for 30 centuries and more. All he knew were boils and pain and financial disaster and personal tragedy and "friends" who didn't understand. He never heard the cheers and shouts from a million worlds as the production he starred in moved toward its climax—"You can do it, Job! Hang in there!"

He never heard the intake of breath across a million galaxies as they waited to see whether, under Satan's brutality, Job would curse God. When his faith broke through at last—"Though He slay me, yet will I trust Him" (Job 13:15, NKJV)—the universe erupted! A million worlds wobbled in orbit at the shock waves of the cheers! His name on a billion lips—"Job! Job! You did it!"

Job's name means "one persecuted." But I wonder whether that new name to be given him on the sea of glass might not mean "one vindicated."

The last chapter of Job's book explains that God "blessed the latter days of Job more than his beginning" (Job 42:12, NKJV). Now there is an act of God!

A millennium later the ancient lesson in God's true relationship to humanity had been forgotten, and the earth was dark with fear of God. Great sufferers were believed to be great sinners. The disciples asked the Messiah, "Who did sin, this man, or his parents, that he was born blind?" "Neither," Jesus replied (John 9:2, 3). Go ahead, ask Him your question: "Those 3,000 upon whom the towers in New York City fell, were they greater sinners than all others in the city?" His answer: "I tell you no!" (see John 9).

Yes, God had the power to save the 3,000. He had the power to save the astronauts who died in the space shuttle disasters, or those who died when the towers fell. He could have halted the Holocaust.

But He didn't.

God has only one Son without sin, but He has no son without suffering—not even Jesus. It must have been hard for Jesus to hang on the cross knowing that He had the power to come down. It must have been hard for the Father too, for He had the power to take Him down. But He didn't.

It was accusation against God that first brought discord into the harmony of the universe. "God, You don't really care for us. You want to rule, to dominate, to crush!" And so He chose to be crushed, so that all the universe might know how much He cares for His creation. He took on Him the sins of us all—

all the distorted notes that our insanity has recorded on the stone of Calvary's hill and on the beams of Calvary's cross. As the darkness of separation from His Father closed about Him, He cried out, "My God, My God, why have You forsaken Me?"

Near my daughter Sherry's left eye is a scar, caused by a swing hitting her when she was 4. I took her to the emergency room and held her down while the doctor wrapped her in a restraining sheet, covering her face. As the doctor worked, forcing a needle that looked as big as a spike into the flesh around her eye, she struggled desperately for release. And she cried out, "Daddy! Daddy!" There was such a world of meaning in those words. Why are you doing this to me? "Daddy! I hurt! I hurt!"

And my hands held her there.

On the cross Jesus cried, "My God! My God! Why have You forsaken Me!" And my hands held Him there. Your hands. Your sins. We held Him there and crushed out His life! Thank God for the shout of triumph that shattered silence, opened graves, shook the earth—"It is finished!" Do you understand what that shout means? Your salvation is assured. Your victory over wrong thoughts, wrong habits. He won the victory for you. It's yours. All you have to do is claim it.

"It is finished!" The whole rotten world order is finished. Wars. Riots. Revolution. The drug culture. Las Vegas. Cheating. Lying. The whole world order. They're all washed up, but the world doesn't know it yet. We've been put here to get the word out.

A little girl always thanked God for something at her evening prayers. Her mother asked her one night, "What are you going to thank God for tonight?"

"For my bump."

"Why would you thank God for that?"

"Because now He can make it well," she replied, and rolled over, closed her eyes, and, we must assume, went peacefully to sleep.

What this child intuitively knew is something that even pastors have to relearn from time to time.

When I first heard of Jim Conway, he was pastor of the Twin City Bible church in Urbana, Illinois. He was married and the father of two teenage girls. Like most pastors, he spent a lot of time comforting the afflicted. His approach was the usual in charismatic churches: "Only believe." "Ask, and you shall receive."

Then he found that his youngest daughter, Becki, had a malignant tumor on her left leg, just above the knee. So he laid hands on her leg and asked God to take the tumor away *right now!* Pastor Conway concluded his prayer and asked Becki, "Is it still there?"

She touched her leg above the knee. "It's still there, Dad."

The next morning Jim asked the doctor to check the tumor before he took out instruments to cut off her leg. He promised that he would. Forty-five minutes later he was still in the operating room, and Jim says, "I knew, I knew." Two hours and 45 minutes later the doctor came out of surgery and told the Conways that he had taken Becki's leg off above mid-thigh. And in his anguish, Jim says, he cried out to God, "WHY! For what reason, God, did You let a beautiful girl have her leg cut off when You could have stopped it? She's only 16! She's only a junior in high school."

Says Conway: "My world had fallen apart. My confidence in God was gone. I found myself beating the wall and saying, "God, where are You! Are You too busy finding a Christian a parking place to care for a girl who was having her leg cut off?

"I had told my daughter that her leg would never

come off. For 25 years I had told people that God is real. That He cares for us individually. That He intervenes in events of life. I had repeatedly claimed the promise from the Bible: 'Ask, and you shall receive'—and now I stood there empty-handed."

Conway's church members tried to comfort him. Said one, "Maybe God is bringing this about in your life because you preach too much on the love of God. Maybe He wants you to preach on His justice."

Jim answered, "You mean that God would chop off my daughter's leg in order to modify my preaching? You and I are following two different Gods—and I don't like yours."

Other well-meaning members told him that perhaps Becki had lost her leg in order to bring the church together. And Pastor Jim answered, "If God has to chop off my daughter's leg in order to bring the church together, and that unity wears off in six months or a year, is He going to chop off her other leg? Then after a year or so take an arm? There isn't enough of Becki to keep any church glued together."

Becki hasn't let the operation change her lifestyle. She bicycles, runs, dates. Friends say she is even more caring and sensitive than before the operation. Recently she was selected homecoming queen of Urbana High School. Her trial has given her intimacy with God and openness to talk about His amazing grace.

And what of her father? Says Jim: "I reduced my frustration and resentment at last to a question: Am I going to demand answers, or am I going to trust God? I decided to let God be God."

Everyone knows that parents are sometimes judged by the behavior of their children. So how does God look through those who bear His name? After all, the Bible is filled with the failures of those who professed to be His. The answer depends on whether we have accepted the "new heart" He offers: "I will give you a new heart. . . . I will put my spirit within you and make you . . . careful to observe my decrees" (Ezekiel 36:26, 27, NAB). The result: "Give ear, O heavens, while I speak," begins the Song of Moses. "Let the earth hearken to the words of my mouth! . . . For I will sing the Lord's renown. Oh, proclaim the greatness of our God! The Rock—how faultless are his deeds; how right are all his ways! A faithful God, without deceit, how just and upright he is!" (Deuteronomy 32:1-4, NAB).

You see, we are part of something big. The universe out there knows us. We are, as Paul says, "a spectacle to the universe, to angels and men alike" (1 Corinthians 4:9, NAB). How we fight in our little shell-pocked foxhole *matters* in this great and grave crisis that sin has visited upon the universe. Inhabitants of other worlds are watching. And when in the name of Jesus we claim our victory, when with Job we testify to our confidence in Him—"though He slay me, yet will I trust Him"—the universe erupts with cheers! "You did it! You did it! You hung in there! You made God look good!"

What a challenge! But that's the challenge we take when, through baptism, we profess our death to sin and accept the new life God is so eager to give us!

Someone once asked me, "If you were accused of being a Christian, would there be enough evidence to convict you?"

A Roman Catholic priest came to my office one day with a manuscript. A native of Poland, he had been researching victims of the Holocaust. He came to tell me of a Sophie Gargasz, age 44, a Seventh-day Adventist, and her husband, Jakub Gargasz, age 62, a Roman Catholic. They lived in Brzozow, a town in southern Poland. On November 19, 1942, three years after the German invasion of Poland, the lampposts and walls of Brzozow were plastered with posters announcing in three languages—German, Ukrainian, and Polish—that anyone who gave food, shelter, or other aid to a Jew would be put to death. It was no empty threat. In a nearby county 24 Polish farmers paid with their lives for harboring 150 Jews. Entire villages were burned with their inhabitants for sheltering one Jew. Imagine what Sophie must have thought when a Jewish woman knocked at her door. Her husband was not home. She had to make her choice alone—expose herself and her husband to the death penalty or ask the woman to leave.

Sophie didn't hesitate. She invited the woman in. When her husband came home, he agreed: they would not turn her from their door. As was to be expected, the gestapo learned of Sophie's act of mercy. She and her husband were arrested and brought before a special tribunal. The proceedings of the court are a matter of record. They were signed by three judges—Pooht, Stumpel, and Aldenhoff on April 19, 1944. Both Sophie and Jakub were sentenced to death.

By her selfless actions Sophie let her light so shine before her executioners that God proved His goodness through her.

If people are asking, "Where are You, God?" maybe it's not because He is hiding, but because we are blocking the view. If people are turning their backs on Him, it may be because they've never seen Him in us. Can we ever really make God look good, unless we too kneel in Gethsemane—kneel to pray, to bleed, and in the face of trials and suffering to say, "Nevertheless, not my will but Thine be done"?

I faced this question once. Soon after we boarded a ship for appointments in Newfoundland, my wife, Stella, began to suffer severe pain in her abdomen. I guessed the reason: an ectopic pregnancy, in which the fertilized ovum develops outside the uterus, as in a fallopian tube. Just a few weeks before, a missionary wife had died in two hours from that condition. The trip to Newfoundland took four hours. The ship captain called ahead for a doctor to meet the ship. I knelt beside Stella and prayed.

The doctor who met the ship reeked of alcohol. After a cursory examination, he asked whether she was always "this white," and told me to take her on to a hospital in Corner Brook, nearly 60 miles away over brutally rough roads. (I learned later that a helicopter had been available at our landing site.) I was driving a Volkswagen Beetle. In it, besides my wife and me, were my mother and our two preschoolers. When we reached Corner Brook four hours later, Stella was near death. The surgeon who examined her turned and ran toward the operating room, shouting "Prepare for an operation, quick!"

A nurse intercepted him to say, "Doctor, we can't—"

He swore at her, and shouted for aides.

I left our children with my mother and went into the hospital chapel. There I knelt and asked God to spare my wife's life. I spoke of our children and their need of their mother; of my decades of work for Him, which had taken me to one place or another in the world for nearly 130 days a year. I spoke of how much I loved and needed my wife.

And then, in a voice that spoke quietly in my mind, God asked me a question: "Are you willing to trust her to Me for My decision?"

How often had I urged people in my circumstance to simply let God be God!

"I trust You, Lord," I said at last. "You know best. I surrender her to You for Your decision."

Suddenly I was flooded with assurance. The sensation was that of kneeling under a dark cloud, and then feeling the warmth of the sun peeking over it. I jumped to my feet and ran toward the operating room. The doctors were just wheeling her in. I clutched her hand. "Oh, Stella," I said, "it's going to be all right!" Yes, whatever God's verdict, it would be all right. Four hours later I was holding her hand when she regained consciousness. Ten days later she flew into New York, where the children and I met her at the airport with a wheelchair.

Since that day God has given me the trust to put not only Stella but our three children into His arms. And God has been generous with forgiveness. He has, however, left me with one probing question that has more than once put me on my knees: Can God ever really shine through us if we carry no cross to our Calvary?

## Chapter 7

# THE GREATEST SIN

One night, long ago, while driving through the flat delta land of southwestern Mississippi, I ran out of gas. That the gas gauge had read empty for 20 miles hadn't concerned me; I knew there was plenty left to get me to the next town. I knew that right up to the time the engine sputtered, and I coasted to a stop by a little unpainted tenement shack. I aroused the family and asked where I could get gas. The father offered to drive me to a station at a nearby town.

When we returned, I found the whole family up, talking to my wife and children. There were eight children in the family, three sets of twins, aged 3, 5, and 8, and two older children. The mother and father and the older children worked in the fields from daylight until dark for a pittance when they could get work. The four youngest stayed at home in the care of the 8-year-olds.

"I dread the thought of fire," the mother said, "but there is nothing else we can do. We just trust in the Lord to spare our children."

I looked at the two 3-year-olds. Lovely children, but small for their age. Their mother must have interpreted my look. "We have a pretty hard time getting them the kind of food they should have."

I looked at my 4-year-old son—husky, happy. He'd never missed a good nutritious meal in his life. I looked at their two little sons. I was still seeing them as I drove away into the coolness of that Mississippi evening. And somehow I knew, as never before, that when I stand in judgment before my Lord, He will not ask me whether I attended church. He will not ask me to pass a test on Bible theology, for far too many "Christians" who are theologically solid are spiritually hollow. I will be asked how much I loved, how selflessly I served God's needy children. Says the Scripture, "Inasmuch as ye have done it unto one of the least of these, my brethren, ye have done it unto me" (Matthew 25:40).

John told it as it is: "Here is the clear difference between God's children and the Devil's children: anyone who does not do what is right or does not love his brother is not God's child. The message you heard from the very beginning is this: we must love one another" (1 John 3:10, 11, TEV).

The fact that I have not killed, committed adultery, blasphemed, stolen—as regards the letter of the law—will not gain me entrance. Against the good works that I have done will be balanced what I might have done. How important it will be, then, that I have confessed my sins of neglect, my lack of self-sacrificing love, and turned my life over to One who so loved that He took the responsibility for my sins and paid my penalty on Calvary's cross.

"Dear friends," writes John, "let us love one another, because love comes from God. Whoever loves is a child of God and knows God. Whoever does not love does not know God, for God is love. And God showed his love for us by sending his only Son into the world, so that we might have life through him. This is what love is: it is not that we have loved God, but that he loved us and sent his Son to be the means by which our sins are forgiven" (1 John 4:7-10, TEV).

I have chosen to emphasize these inspired words of the apostle because I am convinced that the inhumanity of human beings to other human beings is our greatest sin. Lovelessness is the taproot of all human ills. Consider that One who is our example of service. Trying to explain the meaning of His love for mankind, the apostle could find no adequate language to express it, so he said simply, "Behold what manner of love the Father has bestowed upon us, that we should be called children of God" (1 John 3:1, NKJV).

There was no building in Palestine large enough to hold the multitudes that thronged to Christ for healing. And no one who sought Him went away disappointed. On the green hilltops of Galilee, in the thoroughfares of travel, by the seashore, in the synagogues, and in every other place where the sick could be brought to Him was His hospital. In every city, every town, every village through which He passed, He laid hands on the afflicted and healed them.

Christ's life on earth was one of constant self-sacrificing love. He had no home in this world, except as the kindness of friends provided for Him. Wherever He went the tidings of His mercy preceded Him. Where He had passed, the objects of His compassion rejoiced in health. His voice was the first sound many had ever heard; His name the first word they had ever spoken. His face the first they had ever looked upon. Why should they not love Him! As He passed through the towns and villages, He was like a vital current, diffusing life and love and joy. He recognized no distinction of nationality or rank or creed. He set the pattern for a faith in which there is no caste; in which Jew and Gentile, master and slave, rich and poor, are linked in a common brotherhood, equal before God. He passed no one by as worthless.

This, then, is the Man, the life, the love that John asks us to behold and to emulate.

There are four levels on which we may respond to His appeal:

**Antipathy.** This is the level of active hate. It is the I'll-cut-him-down-to-my-size level. It is the level of every person who robs another of dignity and self-worth. It is the level John had in mind when he wrote: "If we say we love God, but hate others, we are liars" (1 John 4:20, TEV).

It is the level of the thieves in the parable of the good Samaritan. A certain man, you'll recall, went down from Jerusalem to Jericho. He was attacked by thieves, who stripped him of his clothing, wounded him, and departed, leaving him "half dead" (Luke 10:30). In our day, you'll find similar stories from home and abroad in virtually every newspaper and on television newscasts.

**Apathy.** This is the level of a person who is indifferent to the needs of fellow beings. It is the level of the priest in the parable, who saw the man beaten by thieves, and who, when he saw him, "passed by on the other side" (verse 31). Apathetic. Indifferent.

In family relationships it is the level of a Carlyle. To be sure, he loved his wife. But he neglected her. He was too busy writing, too absorbed in his work, to show her consideration. After her death he found her diary and read page after page of longing. She had craved the touch of her husband's hand, a kind word, anything but indifference. Carlyle went, too late, to spend bitter days of self-recrimination at her grave. He retired from public life and wrote little, but in a letter to Emerson he reminisced: "Bright, heroic, tender, true, and noble was that lost treasure of my heart, who faithfully accompanied me in all the rocky ways and climbings; and I am forever poor without her." His diary recorded these words: "Oh, that I had you yet for five minutes by my side, that I might tell you all."

The apathy level is also that of the ease-loving Christian, who sees the world's need, sorrows for it, only to pass by on the other side. The prophet Amos drew a word picture of such a person: "Woe to you who are at ease in Zion. . . . Woe to you who . . . lie on beds of ivory, stretch out on your couches, eat lambs from the flock and calves from the midst of the stall; . . . but are not grieved for the affliction of Joseph" (Amos 6:1-6, NKJV).

Is the picture familiar? Surely it is one of luxury. It features people who are building ever bigger houses with ever bigger clothes closets—in which, strangely enough, they put ever scantier clothing. . . . Outside there's a new luxury automobile with a boat beside it.

Don't get nervous. The Lord has nothing against a nice home, a new car, or a boat. His concern is for those who profess to be His but who ignore needs that they are able to—and should—meet. It's lack of love and faith that breaks the Lord's heart.

Apathy. Ever the curse of a people once, twice, removed from their heritage. Shall it be written of us, as Gibbon wrote of the Greeks of Constantinople: "They held in their lifeless hands the riches of their fathers, without inheriting their spirit"?

There is a third, higher level of concern for humanity that characterizes many of us:

**Sympathy.** Sounds nice. Certainly it is laudable to enter into and share the feelings of another. But if sympathy is not accompanied by action, if burdens are not lifted, this level too is worthless. For it is the level of the Levite in Jesus' parable of the good Samaritan. He came and looked sympathetically on his unfortunate fellow traveler. But he too passed him by. The apathetic priest did not even offer a compassionate glance. But was the unfortunate Levite aided by one more than the other? Not one whit! Sympathy that bears no burdens, that knows no sacrifice, that ministers, if at all, without love, is cursed of heaven, even as antipathy and apathy are. In the great judgment day those who have drifted along, carrying no responsibility, thinking of themselves, pleasing themselves, will be placed by the Judge with those who did evil. They receive the same condemnation: "He that does not love does not know God, for God is love."

The Creator made His human creatures with not only the capacity for love but also the necessity. That means that without love, we die. A motion picture shown at the Health Education Conference in New York City's Academy of Medicine depicted the record of the tragic death of 34 infants who had been separated from their parents and placed in a home for children. They had adequate food, clothing, medical attention, and competent and sympathetic nursing. However, each nurse had to care for 10 infants. They had everything they needed, except a mother. Within three months they showed loss of appetite and inability to sleep, and they had vacant expressions. At five months they were shrunken, whimpering, and trembling. A few weeks later 34 were dead. The social workers and physicians who saw the film wept as they watched the babies die, because they had everything they wanted or needed—except a mother.

"Behold, what manner of love the Father has bestowed upon us" (1 John 3:1). I'm speaking of the love represented by the final level on which we can respond to the world's needs. Psychiatrists call it *empathy*. Perhaps, in terms of Christianity, we could call it

**Gethsemane.** This is the level of experimental religion—the level of the Samaritan who saw the unfortunate victim, had compassion on him, and "went to him, and bound up his wounds, . . . and set him on his own beast, and brought him to an inn, and took care of him" (Luke 10:34).

Let's contemporize it. Let's say you're on your way to a town near you. On the way you see a man lying beside the road. You have three choices:

1. Glance at him and drive on. It's really none of your concern.

2. Look, and hope somebody stops to help him.

3. Stop, administer first aid; call for help on your cell phone, and then, noting his itinerary, make reservations for him at the local Holiday Inn. You give the receptionist your credit card number and tell her to care for him until he is able to travel.

By doing so, you have practiced empathy. My seminary teacher described it as "two hearts tugging at one load." Even our cynical and self-centered age holds such compassion in high regard!

Writer Elsie Robinson once visited an old bachelor friend, a famous adventurer and writer. His house was crammed with treasures collected from every part of the world. After she had seen it all, she asked: "Out of all this beauty, what have you cherished most? Which one object is the dearest to you?"

"He gave me a strange look," she writes, "and for a while did not answer. Then he arose and, from its place beneath a priceless Persian tapestry he took a plain bronze box and laid it on my lap. Slowly he raised the lid. Surely I would see something rare and beyond price. Jewels, maybe? Black pearls and fire opals? But no! Here lay only some faded folds of patched blue-and-white gingham—somebody's discarded apron!

"Perhaps I was rude, for I gasped my amazement. 'But what on earth made you keep this, Len?'

"He touched the old cotton with gentle hands,

then he answered softly, 'It was my mother's kitchen apron. And if I had to choose what I would cherish most of all my treasures, I would choose this.'

"And suddenly, as though the years had rolled away, I saw how it had been. He was talking in snatches, but behind the talk I was seeing an old farmhouse kitchen, a busy mother, and a little lad clinging to her apron.

"What a hard-worked apron! Patches across the top where years of dishwashing had worn through the original fabric. Smeared with cookie and flapjack batter. Fragrant with cinnamon and cloves. And spotted from belt to hem with the imprint of a little hand—a toddler to whom that apron represented all the sweetness and security in the world.

"His mother's apron. Yes, surely if he had to lose all the rest of his collection, he would keep this!

"I knew. How well I knew. For through the glaze of tears I was seeing again my own mother and feeling my clutch at her. And all the millions like her, drudging, unsung, yet holding our world together with their apron strings. . . . And then I put my face on the old apron and let the tears come. For now I could realize what I did not understand in my own young, busy years. For once I too wore just such an apron and resented the weary grind of the daily chores. But now I know the glory that rose above the grind, and feel again the little hands that went away so long ago."

This mother's apron, as an emblem of love, of service, of sacrifice, is exceeded by only one thing in all this world—the cross of Calvary on which the Prince of glory died. And everyone who professes the name of Christ professes that highest love, that Gethsemane love. To profess less is to bear false witness against the Christ of Calvary and to mark down the cost of His sacrifice. Up there, maybe while I'm taking a walk by the river of life, I hope you'll introduce yourself and tell me of the day you determined to represent the Prince of glory on the highest level of relationship—empathy. Two hearts tugging at one load. Your heart and the heart of that One who would have died for you had there never been another person in all the world.

## Chapter 8

# OUT OF THE SILENT PLANET

*"Soon we shall look upon the great clock that measures this madness between two eternities, and time shall be no more."*

In his allegorical book *Out of the Silent Planet* English writer and theologian C. S. Lewis conjured up life on Mars and transported several earthlings there by spaceship. One of them, named Ransom, discovers a giant map of the solar system carved into the wall of a temple. He locates the Sun and Mercury. In a niche of the planet stands a winged figure with a trumpet. The next planet, Venus, likewise is dominated by a figure with a trumpet. With mounting excitement he looks at the niche for Earth. The globe representing it is there, but where the flamelike figure should have been is only a deep irregular cut, as if someone has sought to erase Earth's representative.

Later an angel explains. "Earth is the world we do not know. It alone is outside the heaven, and no message comes from it. . . . It was not always so. Once we knew the god of your world—he was brighter and greater than I. . . . It is the longest of all stories and the bitterest. He became bent. . . .

"Those were the Bent Years of which we still speak in the heavens, when he was not yet bound to [Earth] but free like us. It was in his mind to spoil other worlds beside his own. . . . There was a great war, and we drove him back out of the heavens and bound him in the air of his own world. . . . We know no more of that planet. It is silent. We think that [God] would not give it up utterly to the Bent One, and there are stories among us that he has taken strange counsel and dared terrible things, wrestling with the Bent One. It is a thing we desire to look into."

Here, on the Silent Planet, Lewis's words evoke graphic imagery—of war in the heavens, of the dragon, "that ancient serpent called the devil, or Satan, who leads the whole world astray. He was hurled to the earth, and his angels with him. Then I heard a loud voice in heaven say: . . . 'rejoice, you heavens and you who dwell in them! But woe to the earth and the sea, because the devil has gone down to you! He is filled with fury, because he knows that his time is short'" (Revelation 12:9-12, NIV).

He knows. Do we?

Follow me as I explore (1) the certainty of Christ's return; (2) the ambivalence of our expectations; (3) the imminence of His arrival; and (4) the coming of the Bridegroom.

## The Certainty of Christ's Return

Millions of Christians believe that God has not surrendered this one lost world to the Bent One. As Jesus said when He walked on earth as one of us: "I will come again" (John 14:3). Not "I might come again." Not "It is My intention to return." Not "Look for Me when you see Me coming." No. "I WILL come again."

More than 300 references to Christ's second advent are found in the New Testament. Strangely, however, despite these promises from headquarters, most churches no longer believe that Jesus will literally return, despite a heavenly messenger's assurance: "The kingdoms of this world have become the kingdoms of our Lord, and of his Christ; and he shall reign for ever and ever" (Revelation 11:15).

But if He doesn't come, which of His other promises can be believed? That there will be a resurrection of the dead? Jesus said the dead in Christ are to be resurrected when He returns: "For the Lord himself shall descend from heaven with a shout, with the voice of the archangel, and with the trump of God; and the dead in Christ shall rise first" (1 Thessalonians 4:16). If there's no Second Advent, there's no resurrection. As Paul says: "If Christ was not raised, then neither our preaching nor your faith has any meaning at all. Further it would mean that we are lying in our witness for God, for we have given our solemn testimony that he did raise up Christ. . . . And if Christ did not rise your faith is futile and your sins have never been forgiven. Moreover those who have died believing in Christ are utterly dead and gone" (1 Corinthians 15:14–18, Phillips).

If Jesus is not returning, then (1) our preaching is meaningless; (2) our faith is futile; (3) we are liars; (4) our sins have never been forgiven; (5) those who have died believing in Christ are "utterly dead and gone."

## The Ambivalence of Our Expectations

Although the silent prayer of our heart may be "Thy kingdom come," I suspect it is often qualified with "but please, Lord, don't rush it." When as a young man I learned of the return of Christ, I had mixed emotions. First, I knew I was not ready to look God in the face. Someone who realizes his sinful condition, his addiction to sin, does not really look forward to being bathed in the consuming radiance of the Holy One.

And who really wants to go to heaven, anyway? Not that we believe you play harps all day and dangle your feet over clouds. It's just that, well, there are, so far as theologians have been able to determine, very few of the things we've learned to appreciate down here. There are no soap operas there, no yellow front bookstores, no football games, no Dallas cheerleaders, no wine coolers, no Saks Fifth Avenue, no place where you can slip away to do your own thing—unless you really look forward to working in a garden.

Another thing: In my teens I cultivated a deep appreciation of women—as someone called them, "the best other sex we've got." But in Bible class I learned that it was "hands off" until marriage. And that hands-off policy left me most envious of the young married couples on campus. I had heard that in heaven everyone will live together as brother and sister, and I wanted at least a few years of married bliss here. (Actually, theologians say, relationships there are likely to be "heavenly" in comparison to relationships here. And just to stand in the presence of God is likely to be a thrill superseding any sexual or other experience we've had on earth.)

Yes, hurry back, Lord, but not while our hormones are still perking, our arteries relatively free of plaque, we can afford a BMW (or at least a Honda Accord), we're on track for admission to med school, we have no pronounced physical deformities, and the church insists only that we show nominal signs of spiritual life. Of course, if death has intruded into our family, if cells are rioting within us, or if perchance we've come to enjoy the company of Christ and are deep-breathing the atmosphere of heaven, the transition to the new earth does have its attractions.

## The Imminence of His Arrival

As the celestial odometer rolls inexorably forward in these early days of the twenty-first century, millions around the world are looking to signs in the sun and the moon and the stars, as they speculate that this century will bring restored communication between the Silent Planet and the sons and daughters of God throughout the universe. Political and religious leaders alike are speaking somberly of a world turned upside down and about to expire. One told me by letter that the world would end on January 1. His mathematical computations were impressive. I responded by letter. On the envelope I wrote: "Not to be opened until January 2."

Ask almost any Bible student which chapter of the Bible tells us the most about the time of Christ's return and the reply likely will be "Matthew 24." That chapter does indeed list signs of Christ's return. Signs in the heavens. Abounding iniquity. Betrayal. Hatred of the righteous. Counterfeit christs. Yet most of what readers would list as signs are followed by a most significant and little-quoted clause: "But the end is not yet" (verse 6). False christs shall arise—but the end is not yet. You're going to hear the noise of battles close by and the news of battles far away. "Such things must happen, but they do not mean that the end has come. . . . There will be famines and earthquakes everywhere" (verses 6, 7, TEV). But the end is not yet.

I was once to speak to a group of ministers in Missouri. The meeting was canceled, and students were sent home for two days. Why? Because a scientist in San Francisco had predicted that an earthquake would occur on December 4 or 5. I was told that the scientist had not missed on one of his previous seven predictions, including a recent devastating earthquake in San Francisco and one in southern California.

Truth is, the tapes of the scientist's talks show that he made no definite predictions. Rather, he said, "Any day now," or "Sometime in the near future." But schools closed and meetings were canceled based on alleged statements. It didn't matter that not one other scientist specializing in earthquakes agreed. As children of God await the returning Lord, they should remember: "All these things must come to pass, but the end is not yet" (verse 6).

One evening I watched the starlit sky. The moment was neither night nor day. Far in the northwest a light appeared, brighter than a second-magnitude star. Like some celestial messenger mounted on a movable throne, a satellite wrote its way across the sky and was gone. Some saw it and praised the gods of steel and aluminum and liquid oxygen and nitrate, who beam their messages to humanity. But few interpret correctly the fateful finality of that sign in the heavens, for those satellites are forwarding heavensent mail: "And this gospel of the kingdom shall be preached in all the world for a witness unto all nations, and then shall the end come" (verse 14). When the gospel is broadcast to the whole world, Earth's time is up.

The revelator amplifies the message: "Fear God, and give glory to him, for the hour of his judgment is come: and worship him that made heaven, and earth, and the sea, and the fountains of waters" (Revelation 14:7). Why the reference to "fountains of waters"? Is it not evocative of earth's destruction by the Genesis flood, when the "fountains of the deep" burst forth? As I contemplate the incredible apathy of this age of science and séance, I think of two lines by Savinus, written when the Goths had been in Rome and the Vandals were in Carthage: "The Roman Empire is filled with misery, but it is luxurious; it is dying, but it laughs."

Where others see only the silvery trail of an up-thrust rocket, can we not discern the tracings of a down-thrust hand tracing a message of judgment to come upon a vast celestial-domed Belshazzar's hall? Can we not discern that a final editing is even now being given all the works of earthlings by One seated upon a throne high and lifted up, because He has appointed a day in which He will judge the world? Once before, the Lord looked down upon Babel builders, who reached for the heavens, and He said: "This is only the beginning of what they will do; and nothing that they propose to do will now be impossible for them. Come, let us go down" (Genesis 11:6, 7, RSV). To these words from Genesis append the words of Revelation, apt for an age in which humans have for the first time gained the capacity to destroy their world: "Come, let us go down," and "destroy them which destroy [or corrupt] the earth" (Revelation 11:18). The heavens do indeed signal the imminence of the second coming of Christ.

But a caution: For several reasons signs should not be the great motivator in our preparation for Christ's return.

First, signs motivation is generally fear motivation. "The shortness of time is frequently urged as an incentive for seeking righteousness and making Christ our friend. This should not be the great motive with us; for it savors of selfishness. Is it necessary that the terrors of the day of God should be held before us, that we may be compelled to right action through fear? It ought not to be so. Jesus is attractive. He is full of love, mercy, and compassion. He proposes to be our friend, to walk with us through all the rough pathways of life. . . . It is our privilege to have a daily calm, close, happy walk with Jesus" (Ellen G. White, in *Signs of the Times,* Mar. 17, 1887).

The second problem with signs is that no one knows the actual day and hour. As Jesus said, "You must be on the alert then, for you do not know on what day your master is coming" (Matthew 24:42, Phillips). Jesus then told the stories of the faithful servant and the foolish and faithful bridesmaids. The foolish lacked oil in their lamps. The oil did not stand for signs; it represented relationship with Christ. Some had it; some didn't. But when the Bridegroom came, it was too late to get it. The message is, live every day as if it were your last. But not fearfully. *Expectantly!*

To live in expectation of signs raises a third problem, one Jesus addresses early in Matthew 24—deception. Let's look at two aspects: A counterfeit rapture and a counterfeit christ, or antichrist, as he's also called.

**The counterfeit rapture.** The first warning Jesus gave His disciples (see Matthew 24) was against false christs, many of whom, He said, would come. One who did, Bar Kokhba, emerged from the desert to lead 500,000 Jews to their death. In verse 22 Jesus looks through the centuries to warn "the elect" of the end-time against false prophets and false christs who would show "great signs and wonders; insomuch that, if it were possible, they shall deceive the very elect" (verse 24). Our safety, Jesus emphasized, depends on reading and heeding what He has told us (see verse 25).

And now comes a strange warning: "If people should tell you [the elect], 'Look, he [Jesus] is out in the desert' [as Bar Kokhba was]—don't go there; or if they say, 'Look, he is hiding here' [that is, if you are told that He has come secretly]—don't believe it" (verse 26, TEV).

*Do you see? Jesus warns Christians not to be fooled by news that Jesus has returned secretly to snatch away His saints—*referred to by contemporary writers as the "secret rapture." It is in part to highlight this deception that Jesus emphasizes the "public" nature of His return. Don't be fooled by a "secret coming," He urges, because "the Son of Man will come like the lightning which flashes across the whole sky from the east to the west" (verse 27, TEV).

Still, in the face of such a fateful warning, millions of Christians—mostly those who call themselves Evangelicals—anticipate a secret coming. I've examined some 20 current books on the secret rapture written by such well-known authors as Hal Lindsey and Tim LaHaye. Millions of their books have been sold, and millions of readers are being deceived.

Let's imagine their scenario: It's Sunday morning, and you've slept in. You meander to the kitchen for your morning cup, you pick up the TV remote, and your tranquillity departs as you view the morning news. Your favorite reporter is shaking, and within seconds so are you. Well-known personalities have been disappearing all over the world, he says. One charismatic preacher disappeared just as he was making an appeal for $10 million and saying that if he didn't get it, the Lord would take him home. It appears that the Lord may have done so. Another station informs you that two pilots, one on United and one on American, disappeared during flights out of Dallas; copilots landed the aircraft. Reports of cars crashed on beltways and drivers missing from still-fastened seat belts are coming in. Your phone rings, and an excited friend informs you that a pastor on the staff of his church disappeared during the service. Viewers worldwide are hearing similar reports: A member of the British cabinet has vanished; a head of state in Africa is feared kidnapped.

Now you hear the commentators. One Evangelical preacher after another is saying that Jesus has come secretly and snatched up millions of saints. We are told that the rest of us, still on Planet Earth, will have to go through a seven-year period of hell on earth, called the "great tribulation," before Jesus returns to set up His kingdom.

The preachers are quoting the words of Jesus Himself from Matthew 24: "Then shall two be in the field; the one shall be taken, and the other left. Two women shall be grinding at the mill; the one shall be taken, and the other left. Watch therefore: for ye know not what hour your Lord doth come" (verses 40-42). Others are quoting the antichrist passages from chapter 2 of Paul's second letter to the church in Thessalonica.

But when the Bible says that Jesus comes as a thief, it must mean He comes unexpectedly. It cannot mean He comes secretly, because 2 Peter 3:10 says that on that day "the heavens will disappear with a roar; the elements will be destroyed by fire, and the earth and everything in it will be laid bare" (NIV). Nothing secret there! That's the end! As we have noted, there is no secret rapture of the church before Jesus' second coming. "Believe it not," Jesus warns His followers. When Jesus returns, says John, "every eye shall see him" (Revelation 1:7)!

There remains, however, the ultimate deception.

**The counterfeit Christ.** The Bible calls him the antichrist. "Anti" implies not only one who is against Christ, but also one who sets himself up in the place of Christ. Let's note Paul's warning in his second letter to the church in Thessalonica, some members of which were teaching that Christ had already returned in their day:

"Now we implore you, . . . by the certainty of the coming of our Lord Jesus Christ and of our meeting him together, to keep your heads and not be thrown off your balance by any prediction or message or letter purporting to come from us, and saying that the day of the Lord has already come. Don't let anyone deceive you by any means whatsoever. That day [of Christ's second advent] will not come before there first arises a definite rejection of God and the appearance of the lawless man. . . . He even takes his seat in the Sanctuary of God, to show that he really claims to be God" (2 Thessalonians 2:1-4, Phillips).

Paul continues: "Evil is already insidiously at work but its activities are secret until what I have called the 'restraining power' is removed. When that happens the lawless man will be plainly seen—though the words from the mouth of the Lord Jesus spell his doom, and the radiance of his coming will be his utter destruction" (verses 7, 8, Phillips). As might be expected from the name Inspiration has given him, his last vicious attack is against those "who keep the commandments of God and bear testimony to Jesus" (Revelation 12:17, RSV).

"The lawless man is produced by the power of Satan and armed with all the force, wonders and signs that falsehood can devise" (2 Thessalonians 2:9, Phillips).

Notice carefully: In Matthew 24 Jesus warns the elect that the last-day false prophets and false christs shall show "great signs and wonders." Why? Two reasons: First: "If it were possible, they shall deceive the very elect" (verse 24; see also Revelation 13:13, 14). The second reason is transparent: The lawless man comes, as Paul said, "armed with all the force, wonders and signs that falsehood can devise" *to certify his identity as the Messiah!*

"To those doomed to perish," Paul continues, "he will come with evil's undiluted power to deceive [straight demonic vodka!] for they have refused to love the truth which could have saved them" (2 Thessalonians 2:10, Phillips). And who are deceived? "All inhabitants of the earth will worship the beast—all whose names have not been written in the book of life belonging to the Lamb" (Revelation 13:8, NIV). Who will *not* be deceived? "Those who obey God's commandments and hold to the testimony of Jesus" (Revelation 12:17, NIV). Those who "perish," Paul adds, "perish because they refused to love the truth that could have saved them" (2 Thessalonians 2:10, Phillips).

What truth? *That Jesus has not come secretly!* That when He comes, every eye shall see Him! When you are told that Christ has already come secretly, don't believe it! And what if you do? Paul gives the inspired answer: "God sends upon them, therefore, the full force of evil's delusion, so that they put their faith in an utter fraud and meet the inevitable judgment of all who have refused to believe the truth and who have made evil their pleasure" (verse 11, Phillips). It doesn't pay to play games with evil! So Paul addresses those loyal to Christ, "stand firm, and hold on to the teachings we passed on to you" (verse 15, Phillips).

## The Coming of the Bridegroom

The return of Jesus to this Silent Planet is as certain as His other promises. Signs set forth in Scripture indicate His return to be imminent. However long He may delay—out of desperate love for those children who deny their divine parenthood—we must live every day as if we will meet Him before tomorrow. As Paul advises, we must stand firm, and hold loyally to the teachings passed on to us through the Word. All this counsel is embraced in the Lord's directive to the disciples and the elect of end time: "Watch therefore, for you do not know what hour your Lord is coming" (Matthew 24:42, NKJV). Only by watching will we perceive the last great deception; only by daily fellowship with our divine Companion can we survive.

It is my conviction, based on Christ's own prophetic words, that the curtain is being pulled open for the last act in the great drama of the ages. Actors on life's stage are even now sounding their last lines. "Soon we shall look upon that great clock that measures this madness between two eternities, and time shall be no more." It was James Joyce who wrote: "History is a nightmare out of which I am trying to awake." Some bright morning we shall awaken from our dreams to find nothing vanished save our sleep. For God has not given up this world; rather He has dared terrible things wrestling with the Bent One. And soon Earth shall no longer be outside the heavens.

Shall we then fear? Does one fear the coming of a friend? The King is coming! And the King is our friend!

I remember a Christian witnessing group of 55 young people, ages 14 to 26, who sang and witnessed to their faith during the summers. They took no salary, and sometimes didn't even know where they would eat or sleep. One day they sang and witnessed at a luncheon for the contestants and sponsors of the South Carolina beauty pageant in Greenville. Their closing number was a song called "The King Is Coming."

A few days later at a shopping center in Columbia, a young woman stepped up to the group and identified herself as a contestant in the beauty contest. "I just had to tell you what happened after you left us in Greenville," she said. "That night we all decided to pray together. We prayed that the Lord would not let us be self-centered and dissatisfied if we didn't win. We started to pray for each other and become boosters for each other. When we finished the pageant, the officials told us that we were the finest group of young women they had ever had competing for Miss South Carolina. One girl spoke up and told them it was because of the young people who had pointed them to

Christ. To many of us," she said, "He became the most important person in our lives."

A few years back I was in Madrid. A young soldier, Reuben Escribano, had been court-martialed for refusing to dishonor God's Sabbath. His sentence: six years in prison.

I met with a number of youth in the Madrid Adventist Church to pray for Reuben. We knelt in a circle, feeling the spiritual oneness of our prayer quest. The youth asked me to pray last. They thanked God for Reuben's faithfulness and prayed that God would comfort him. They expressed their hope that, in the providence of God, he might be released. Prayer after prayer around the circles ascended to God. Kneeling beside me was a lovely young woman, perhaps 19 or 20 years old. I shall never forget the earnestness of her prayer. I understood Spanish well enough to follow her petition. I did not need Spanish to feel the intensity of her pleading. There was not another sound to be heard. It was as if a Visitor from heaven had slipped into our midst. We sensed His presence and trembled.

Afterward I asked the pastor who the young woman who had opened her heart with such intensity for Reuben was. "Ah," he said, "she is Reuben's fiancé. They were to be married soon."

Then I understood. And I wondered whether I could ever love my Savior with such intensity that I would plead for His return as that young fiancé had pleaded for her lover's. In the years since—as I have enjoyed fellowship with Jesus, as I have basked in the assurance of His finished work at Calvary and thrilled at His commitment to stand for me in judgment—I have sometimes found my yearnings for Him so intense that I've just knelt and silently opened my heart to Him, for no words would suffice.

## Chapter 9

# FAREWELL TO SHADOWLANDS

A few months ago I followed a commercial to Nordstrom's, my wife's favorite department store. Her birthday was nearing, and I envisioned a new spring dress. Second floor had, a clerk told me, the up-to-date spring beauties. So there I went. And there I saw an amazing sight! Near the beautiful dresses of Jones New York, Carol Little, Oleg Cassini, and Liz Claiborne (none of which my wife has in her closet) was a rack of jeans that I assumed must have been put aside for the Salvation Army. Worn. Torn. Faded. I looked at the tag on a pair called Faded Glory. "This garment," it said, "is sewn and professionally laundered to give the look of being old and worn. Flaws and imperfections are a part of the total desired look." The Faded Glory jeans were selling for twice the price of the nearby new-looking jeans! The sales tag sought to reassure me: "Flaws and imperfections are part of the total desired look."

And how does the world get us to buy its "faded glory" (or, as I shall be calling it, "Virtual Reality")? The apostle Paul put it straight: "The god of this world has blinded the minds of those who do not believe" (2 Corinthians 4:4, Phillips). The world has a bill of goods to sell to those who do not perceive Reality to have a thorn-crowned brow.

A baseball player testifies: "Since I accepted Christ, my batting average has gone up 30 points."

Miss Philadelphia says: "I'm glad for what Jesus has done for me since I became a Christian. He has added two inches to my bust and taken away three from my hips."

College student Rip Howell has set a record by lying 17 hours in a tub of ketchup. (I thought you'd like to know.)

Virtual reality. Values out of balance.

"The god of this world has blinded the minds of those who do not believe."

Helen Keller, blind and deaf from infancy, was asked what she thought to be the worst calamity that could befall a person. She replied: "To have eyes and fail to see."

It's not a rare disease, this blindness of soul. If the condition called for white canes, the *tap-tap-tapping* in the aisles of our churches would sound like the Parade of the Wooden Soldiers.

*Virtual reality* is a computer term. And computers often aid and abet in a distortion of reality. Housewife Rita Smith alerted me to it: "We were, my ex-husband once observed wryly, the only family he knew with two modems, three fax machines, and a communication problem." In Rita's case, irony is implicit in her occupation: She runs a communication firm.

Think with me about communications and human relationships on the information highway. In a publication called *Footnotes to the Future,* Roger Shinn suggests the dimension of the communication problem:

"We are living in a world saturated with communication, on the verge of perishing for lack of it; a world smothered with words, hungry for one meaningful word; a world bombarded with data, rarely capable of sorting out the truth; and a world in which we can flash messages across the ocean by way of space, but one in which we find it difficult to get through to each other face to face."

I own two computers—one in my home study, the other for my travels. I edit articles for publication on them. I write books on them. My life has been characterized by deadlines. I wince when I recall the times my wife has tried to pry me away from my desk: "Wouldn't you love to go to Baltimore and spend a few hours with me at the Inner Harbor? We could go to Fort McHenry." "Honey, did you remember that today is our anniversary?" Ouch!

How about you? Own a computer? Ever play games on it? If not, you're likely a grandparent, and your children and grandchildren are playing the games. In fact, millions today are abandoning real life for what computer people call the virtual reality of cyberspace. I know of one player who loved acting out scenarios in what participants called World's End Bar. He posed as a street tough who had been kicked around by life. Then real life beckoned in the person of Dad, who told his son he must get a job. Said Dad: "In order to live the imaginary life, you have to pay dues in real life." And so you do, though that conclusion is not endorsed by millions traversing the movies, videos, television, and arcades of the cyberspace highway.

But, as Rita found, the cost in human relationships is prohibitive. I've had to search my own heart: Am I unwilling to push away from the computer terminal to spend more time with the family I love if it means missing a computer game? Or, as one who seeks to introduce others to the God who calls me His son, dare I waste the time during which I may demonstrate the reality of His genuine goodness through face-to-face relationships? I made a decision to choose a reality that, I believe, exceeds the qualified "virtual" brand.

Nevertheless, in our pursuit of reality, we had better understand how virtual reality differs from the real thing.

Back in the early sixteenth century "virtual" referred to something of moral excellence. Today it means "almost," as for example, "The twins were virtually identical." Maybe only one had a wart on his posterior. In today's context, then, "virtual" describes something that falls just short of being genuine, real, or true. Theologically, it could describe a subtle distortion of life—offering something short of God's vision for us.

Actor Charlie Sheen's experience in his personal World's End Bar highlights the distinction I'm making. Sheen tells of assuming the role of a young movie star who was into money, drugs, wine, cars, women, and partying all night. Says Sheen: "It got so that I couldn't tell where the film world stopped and the real world began." The real world opened up to him, he says, only after he checked into a rehab center.

During my freshman year in college I took a course in photography from a fine professor named Richard Lewis. He emphasized framing a photograph. Artists and photographers use this technique to help them see. To help them pull order out of chaos. The world is too big to see all at once. To make sense of it, we must look at small parts selectively, shutting out the rest much as the photographer does through his or her viewfinder. In short, to define reality correctly, we must frame our world through the viewfinder of God's Word—a viewfinder that reminds us that virtual reality is banishing the face-to-face, heart-to-heart communication and friendship that God desires us to share.

Highlighted in Phillips' dynamic translation of 1 John 3:1, 2 is a devastating analysis of virtual reality, as well as several assertions concerning reality: "Consider the incredible love that the Father has shown us in allowing us to be called, 'children of God'—and that is not just what we are called, but what we are. This explains why the world will no more recognise us than it recognised Christ. Here and now . . . we are God's children." This "real life" (as contrasted to virtual reality) is to be found only in His Son (1 John 5:11). John adds, "Never give your hearts to this world [which represents only virtual reality] or to any of the things in it" (1 John 2:15, Phillips).

Why? Three reasons:

• First, when we accept Christ we become, as Peter has said, only "temporary residents" here (1 Peter 2:11, Phillips). Our fellowship with Christ here and the vision He gives us of the "there" should draw us out of what G. K. Chesterton called "narrow infinities," enabling us to sing with conviction, "I'm but a stranger here; Heaven is my home."

• Second, we must never give our heart to the world, because we cannot love the Father and the world at the same time. God's world has values that differ radically from those of this world, and they are incompatible. Values such as love, respect, virtue, truth, honesty, and purity—all of which differ radically from the values of the "whole world-system," which, says John, "is based on men's desires, their greedy ambitions, and the glamour of all that they think splendid" (1 John 2:16, Phillips).

You'll find a catalog of these "splendid" nonvalues in the *TV Guide,* in movies, in best-seller lists of books and magazines. The world's "holy hedonism" is practiced by the rogues of Wall Street, the shills of Madison Avenue, the practitioners of politics wherever. Make no mistake: Our character takes on the values or nonvalues of the homeland whose passport we carry. And only one homeland offers "permanent" residency.

• Third, when we don't know who our Father is, we can't tell who we are. Columnist Thomas Boswell wrote of young athletes who "often become by 16 uncontrollable, vacuous, and spoiled monsters—incredibly rich, out of touch with reality and utterly without identity when they are not [playing their game]."

When we lose touch with the reality that is Jesus Christ, we also lose self-identity—the concept of who we really are: here and now God's son; here and now God's daughter; here and now part of His own indestructible heredity; here and now loved beyond our comprehension. We must never, never undervalue ourselves! Heaven gave its most precious gift for us. And someday, thanks to what Paul calls God's "glorious generosity" (Ephesians 1:6, Phillips), He will share everything that is His with us—really!

I hope you're as excited as I am by the reality of these wonderful assurances of God's vision for us, His children. I didn't grow up in God's house. He reached out to me in the orphanage of my despair, my alienation, and made me heir to all that is His. When that reality broke through, I found the things of this earth growing strangely dim.

What a wonderful reality! *God adopted me!* Maybe that's why the story of Peter Petkowski means so much to me. Peter, a miserable-looking shell-shocked, malnourished, emotionally stunted 10-year-old, lived through the destruction of Warsaw in World War II. When an American couple, the Johnsons, saw the spindly-legged little boy with the big haunted eyes, they thought he would make a good companion for their son, Donald, age 12.

The warmth and love and tranquillity of the Johnsons' Iowa farmhome worked wonders on Peter's damaged nerves, but it soon became evident that he never would be quite like other children. Unexpected noises brought a thin high-pitched shriek from contorted lips. It would be hours before his body stopped shaking. He couldn't sleep nights: the dark terrified him. School imposed stresses that he couldn't handle.

Donald was the one stable element in Peter's life. He defended Peter from the taunts and cruel humor of his peers. And Peter loved Donald. He followed him about the house and would sit adoringly at his feet. Sometimes the Johnsons would find him in bed with Donald. And at last the nightmares were over.

Then Peter became ill. The doctor diagnosed diphtheria. "Keep Peter away from Donald," the parents were warned. But one night the nightmares returned. Peter seemed to be in Warsaw again; he could hear the Stukas diving on the city; feel the concussion of the bombs. And when the terror overwhelmed him, he crept from his bed and slipped into Donald's room. Mrs. Johnson found him there in the morning, his arms wrapped around their son.

A few days later Donald came down with diphtheria, and a week later he was dead.

A friend from the West Coast came to visit the Johnsons some months after Donald's death. He found Mr. Johnson and Peter working together in the garden. His astonishment and anger spilled out at the sight of the wretched little refugee. "How can you keep this miserable creature?" he demanded. "He cost you your son!"

Mr. Johnson put his arm protectively around Peter's shoulders. "Careful what you say," he told his friend. "You see, you're speaking about my son. We've adopted Peter."

Oh, dear God! What my adoption cost heaven! When the reality of Calvary breaks through, when you feel what C. S. Lewis called the "drippings of grace" falling on your parched soul, you'll never feel lonely again. In God's vision reality is something more than virtual; it's a Person, a Person with nail-pierced hands; it's adoption into the family of God, taking His name and becoming part of His own indestructible heredity.

Still, God is not the only one contending for our loyalty. There is another.

The news was disheartening: A number of students from two major colleges had been dismissed for cheating. Said one student, who didn't want to be named: "Not lying, cheating, or stealing doesn't seem to get you anywhere in this day and age. . . . I wish the administration would wake up and realize that the . . . honor system is a bunch of crap!"

William C. Sullivan, for 10 years head of the FBI's domestic intelligence division, has written: "Scarcely anyone who was involved in the operations—bugging phones, breaking into houses, slipping LSD to unsuspecting bar patrons, planning assassination attempts, undermining governments— seems to have wondered whether he was doing anything wrong. . . . Never once did I hear anybody, including myself, raise the question 'Is this course of action . . . lawful, is it legal, is it ethical or moral?' We never gave any thought to this line of reasoning."

Paul emphasizes the sensual consequences of spiritual blindness in his letter to the Christians in Ephesus: "This is my instruction, then, which I gave you in the Lord's name. Do not live any longer the futile lives of gentiles. For they live in a world of shadows, and are cut off from the life of God through their deliberate ignorance of mind and sheer hardness of heart. They have abandoned themselves to sensuality, practising any form of impurity which lust can suggest" (Ephesians 4:17-19, Phillips).

Why? Because they are blindfolded. You can't have vision when you're blindfolded. Beware: virtual reality can lead you into shadowlands, where evil rubs its whiskers across your cheeks.

Pornographers say that soon, on our TV or computer screen, Miss Centerfold will beckon you to join her on a sofa and tell her what you would enjoy. She'll be able to slink toward you, reach out her hand, and draw you onto a sofa with her, where she'll offer to fulfill your fantasies.

I can anticipate the results. After a few months in computer fantasyland, a generation of young males who have rotted before they've even ripened will either totter forth, scared to death at the thought of an actual physical contact with a living, breathing female, or—even worse—emerge convinced that Miss Centerfold's sexual prowess is what they can expect as their due every day of their married life.

Back to Paul's letter to the Christians in Ephesus: "You have learned nothing like . . . [virtual reality] from Christ. . . . No, what you learned was to fling off the dirty clothes of the old way of living, which were rotted through and through with lust's illusions, and, with yourselves mentally and spiritually re-made, to put on the clean fresh clothes of the new life which was made by God's design for righteousness and the holiness which is no illusion" (verses 20-24, Phillips).

If you've got a blindfold on, tear it off; see the world as it is—with its virtual values, its faded glory. See it as God sees it, not as the god of this world disguises it.

Another problem with unreality: If humanity's dilemma is metaphysical and not moral, morality is only an illusion rooted in the wrong concept of being. There are no moral absolutes. Truth is a chameleon, changing color to whoever views it. Ethics are only ground rules that you or I can make and change during the "game." There is really no good-guy, bad-guy confrontation on Main Street. There are only actors who are best of friends backstage.

But in reality there are absolutes. There is a moral code to live by, and that code is a transcript of the reality of God's character. To live morally is simply to live in harmony with what God is. To sin is to fall short of reflecting His image of love. Thus the apostle John says that when the ultimate reality breaks through, "when he appears we shall be like him, for we shall see him as he is. Everyone who has at heart a hope like that keeps himself pure, as Christ is pure" (1 John 3:2, 3, Phillips). When you see reality as a Person, that vision shapes your character.

To live immorally is to reflect a world of illusion. Surely, then, it is imperative that we determine whether we are among those deluded: Is that inner voice of conscience still transmitting, still warning, still tracking reality—or is there static on the channel?

I had finished a lecture on sex at a Christian university, concluding that when God says no to premarital sex, it is not to deprive us of pleasure but to ensure that we have it in all its dimensions. He who made us more than body knows that two bodies meeting without that meeting of mind and spirit for which our whole being cries is a miserably incomplete experience.

Afterward, Carl confronted me. "What's wrong with going all the way?" he demanded.

"Nothing," I responded. "Nothing at all. You see, the problem is, what you call 'going all the way' isn't. It isn't going even halfway. You're really talking about semi-sex, and that I oppose emphatically."

We eye-wrestled for a few moments, with the youth trying unsuccessfully to hide his rising interest. "OK," he said at last, with a gesture of surrender. "I'm hooked. Haul me in."

"Sex," I told him, "is not a distance you go. It is not just something you do. It is something you and the person you love are becoming together. As God put it: 'These two shall become one.' Sex involves total commitment of two personalities, not just the meeting of two bodies. And you can't go all the way unless the whole being is involved.

"God wrote the commandment prohibiting fornication and adultery not because He wanted to deprive you but because He wanted to make sure you did 'go all the way' in that total involvement of being—physical, mental, and spiritual—that can come only to two people deeply in love and within the security of marriage. Outside marriage, there are always inhibitions: hang-ups. Worries about pregnancy. Worries about being used. Worries about commitments neither party is qualified to fulfill. That is why sex outside of marriage is so often deeply disappointing. It just isn't complete.

"Now tell me, Carl, does it make sense to settle for the physical alone, for semi-sex, when God, the author of sex, invites you to 'go all the way'?"

"Well," he replied, "when you put it that way . . ."

He married soon after. His father shared a note from Carl that he received the night of the wedding. "Dear Dad," it began. "I suppose many dads wonder whether their sons behaved before marriage. You know what I mean. Well, a few months ago Marian and I decided that you really can't go all the way before marriage. Not even if you try. So we waited. See you after the honeymoon. Carl."

Lust says you can satisfy the physical and be

happy. But God's Word says, "No." Reality is not two bodies meeting in a Dodge van called "Passion Pit." Reality is a "Thou shalt not commit adultery." And that provision covers also the private fantasies psychiatrists say provide a "healthy" release for sexual tensions. Jesus said that to lust in the spirit is to commit adultery in fact.

A human being, made in the image of God, is more than body. The Creator designed us with a triple reality—body, mind, and spirit. And then He endowed us with faith, hope, and love, which, the apostle Paul says, last forever! Think of it! Faith in each other. Hope that offers a relationship in which two people may become one, while retaining those God-given attributes of personality and individuality that make each such a special person. "Incredible love," the kind Paul challenges us to "consider the incredible love that the Father has shown us in allowing us to be called 'children of God'—and that is not just what we are called, but what we are" (Hebrews 1:1, Phillips).

If you really want to be Total Woman or Total Man, you'll find the way through union with the reality that is our Creator and Redeemer. Let's see what else His three gifts may offer.

**Faith in God's future.** So Paul writes to Timothy: "Tell those who are rich in this present world . . . not to rest the weight of their confidence on the transitory power of wealth but on the living God. . . . Their security should be invested in the life to come, so that they may be sure of holding a share in the life which . . . is permanent" (1 Timothy 6:17-19, Phillips).

Krister Stendahl said, "Faith is not believing in spite of the evidence; it is obeying in spite of the consequences." It is living in the dark as if the daylight had already come. Faith punches holes in the dark, and stars shine through.

**Then there is hope.** Little Emma was taking an exam in school. She puzzled over one question: "Upon what do hibernating animals subsist during the winter months?" Finally she wrote: "On the hope of a coming spring."

I spoke at the memorial service of a close friend who had died of cancer. The family had a short private service at the grave site. That afternoon, in the church, there was no casket. The family wanted no symbol of death—of "winter"—in the church. Instead they asked for the reality of "spring," and resurrection through the living Word. Hope is the way we express our desire for reality and our expectation of obtaining it. So long as there is anything to be desired and expected, hope will exist. It is an eternal commodity.

**The last of the gifts from the reality to come is love.** But what is love? You can't put it in a cash register and make it ring up paid. "I love chocolate." "I love tennis." In tennis "love" means nothing—as in "the score is 30-love." But the love God holds for us means everything. And of that agape love, that agape reality, we are to partake and share. And when we do, we'll hear the music of eternity sending shivers through the here and now.

Did you know that lovers really do hear music that others don't? Two doctors of Stanford Medical School, who have undertaken the first scientific study of love, say that it is true. Your life changes when you are in love. You go in new directions. You engage in new enterprises. You get in touch with new realities in yourself. Yes, love lets us hear music the earthbound cannot discern. And could we not hear music now, real music, if we listened with our love focused on the reality above—that reality with a face and a smile and arms opened wide for us? Arms that were spread on a cross, hands that knew the pounding of nails. A voice that cried, "Father, forgive them. . . . It is finished!" When He said that, it was this world that faded, the things of this earth that grew strangely dim. "Now we see only puzzling reflections in a mirror," but "there are three things that last for ever—faith, hope, and love" (1 Corinthians 13:12, 13, NEB). They're part of the permanent because they're part of reality, the only reality that counts! "Here and now," writes John, "we are God's children" (1 John 3:2, Phillips). And when "reality" breaks through, Paul adds in his letter to Corinth, "We shall see reality whole and face to face" (1 Corinthians 13:12, Phillips).

Reality has a face! Reality is a person, the Lord Jesus Christ! And we are reality because we are created in His image. We are not just actors on a galaxy-sized Hollywood set. Here and now we are God's children. For the child of God, reality is never freedom from individuality, but freedom at last to be finally and fully oneself.

Not that we become loners. As one writer has expressed it, "We cannot come in touch with divinity without coming in touch with humanity; for in Him who sits upon the throne of the universe, divinity and humanity are combined. Connected with Christ, we are connected with our fellow men by the golden links of the chain of love" (*Christ's Object Lessons,* pp. 384, 385).

Here is the theology that keeps my feet walking in Christ's footsteps, while I reach for the reality that shall be.

During my years as a son of God I've walked in the footsteps of others who have touched divinity.

**Nepal.** A little mission hospital is tucked in the shadow of Mount Everest. I shall never forget the child—perhaps 10 years old—dressed in a faded pink dress and sitting alone in a hospital room. "She has tuberculosis," a nurse told me. I spoke to the young wife of one of the doctors. "It's a lot different from

California," she said. "There we'd go out with friends on Saturday night. Here it's very lonely. But we are here because Jesus told us to walk in His steps. And He was called the "great healer."

**China.** I was in Shanghai with a friend, Dr. Thomas Geraty, who sought the grave of his preschool son, who had died of a childhood affliction that could have been successfully treated in the States. We finally found the area. It had been covered by an aircraft runway.

Two young couples went to China as missionaries. After a few months the two husbands left their wives to seek a site farther into the interior where they might serve. They returned to find that their wives had been hacked to death by Chinese bandits. The bereft husbands sent word of the tragedy to their church headquarters, who, in turn, notified the parents of the young women.

The parents of one of the women sent a reply: "We hope the cause of God has not suffered by this tragedy. If we had another daughter, we would send her; and if we were younger, we would go ourselves." It was signed: "Mr. and Mrs. Martin."

For many years I carried a copy of their response in my billfold. When lonely in some far-off corner of the globe, I would take it out and read it. Then I would go on with my mission.

Yes, many have faced the reality of their mission on Planet Earth, and many have gone into their graves in full confidence of resurrection on some bright morning.

What else can we do if we are to reflect a God who washed feet?

## Chapter 10

# SYMBOLS OF REDEMPTION

As the scruffy youth sauntered along the boardwalk in Santa Monica, California, I saw it on the backseat of his worn and torn pair of Levi shorts—the American flag. Old Glory. I didn't stand at attention. I didn't salute it. If I'd had a paddle, and a smidgen more courage, I'd have whacked his star-spangled rear.

In most countries the authorities would happily have jailed the youth for desecration of the flag. But not in the United States, where the Supreme Court has said that flag desecration is protected by the First Amendment's guarantee of free speech. A few years ago Congress too took this stance. One congressman, however, calling the flag a "unique symbol," said the flag should not be desecrated because "too many people have paid for it with their blood. Too many have marched behind it. Too many have slept in a box under it. Too many kids and parents and widows have accepted this [symbol] as the last remembrance of their most precious loved one. Too many to have this [flag] ever demeaned."

A flag is the symbol of a nation. When we salute the flag, we pledge our loyalty to our homeland. When it is attacked, we rush to its defense. Small wonder we're offended when we see our flag adorning someone's jean-clad posterior, decorating a garbage can, or burning at a protest rally.

And yet a flag is essentially a piece of cloth. Were I to put a match to a piece of blue cloth, a piece of white cloth, and a piece of red cloth, no American, however loyal, would protest. But put them together, link them with stars, and the pieces of cloth become something more than the sum of their parts. They become the symbol of our country.

A day too may be something more than the sum of its parts—the seconds, the minutes, and the hours with which it is sewn together. Birthdays, anniversaries, graduation—these are more than just another day. How much more true of the Sabbath—a unit of time cut from the fabric of eternity itself and given to earthlings by their Creator. When as children of God we weekly observe this symbol of our heavenly homeland, we acknowledge God's creative authority over the embassy of our heart.

Over this symbol, as over the flag, a controversy rages, a controversy with roots in the apostate and intolerant centuries. Adding international currency to the issue is the recent papal encyclical *Dies Domini,* which abandons the centuries-old claim that the Roman Catholic Church has changed the law of God, and attempts a biblical defense for the Christian Sunday.

For several reasons I am thankful for *Dies Domini.* First, it focuses the world's attention on God's symbol of His creative and re-creative powers. Second, it directs us to the Bible for a discussion of the issues. And anyone who comes to the Bible seeking truth about God's Sabbath will soon determine that the papal-anointed day of worship is 24 hours off, and that far more than a matter of hours is at stake. The Bible reveals the seventh-day Sabbath to be (1) a symbol of God's authority, (2) a test of our loyalty, (3) the definer of who and how we are to worship, and (4) God's redemptive assurance that "all things bright and beautiful" shall soon again be ours. Let's examine each scriptural revelation.

## The Sabbath as a Symbol of God's Authority

Uncle Oscar Hegstad, a short bank teller-like person with frameless glasses and a small but determined chin, was the first Sabbathkeeper in our family. My father's oldest brother, he attended an Adventist tent meeting in Devils Lake, North Dakota, way back in "the dear dead days beyond recall." Night after night my Lutheran uncle came home angry, but with every text written down. And night after night he studied them and prayed over them. When the meetings ended, Uncle Oscar was a Seventh-day Adventist, a status that for years was to make him, in the family's estimation, the only nut on the family tree.

During my grade school years in Wauna, Oregon, he was a colporteur. When he'd stop by our home and talk with us about his religious convictions, he was persuasive. I used to love bacon and eggs for breakfast, but after he got done telling me how filthy pork was, I was off it—in all its permutations—for life.

But the Sabbath was another matter. Uncle Oscar could summon science to his side against pork, but not on behalf of the seventh-day Sabbath, which just didn't seem to make sense. First, it seemed as if only a few religious oddballs observed it. Second, it seemed irrational. Most of the other commandments made sense: anybody—Christian or Muslim or Buddhist or atheist—knew that they shouldn't steal, lie, kill. If the Lord had said, "Rest on one day in seven," that would have made sense, because everybody needs rest, and "Sabbath" means rest. But the Sabbath commandment—arbitrarily, it seemed—specified cessation from work on the seventh day:

"Remember the sabbath day, to keep it holy. Six days shalt thou labour, and do all thy work: but the seventh day is the sabbath of the Lord thy God: in it thou shalt not do any work, thou, nor thy son, nor thy daughter, thy manservant, nor thy maidservant, nor thy cattle, nor thy stranger that is within thy gates: for in six days the Lord made heaven and earth, the sea, and all that in them is, and rested the seventh day: wherefore the Lord blessed the sabbath day, and hallowed it" (Exodus 20:8-11). As Uncle Oscar pointed out, "hallowed" means "set apart for holy use."

Of course, the Sabbath is only the fourth of the Ten Commandments. In their universal format— "Thou shalt love the Lord thy God with all thy heart, and with all thy soul, and with all thy strength, . . . and thy neighbour as thyself" (Luke 10:27)—they are a universal "Bill of Rights," pointing the way to eternal happiness. James calls the Ten Commandments the "law of liberty" (James 2:12). Though I was not raised a Christian, I don't recall that either my parents or I had much trouble with the idea that God's got a law—assuming, of course, that He really existed. It did seem logical that any ruler would have a law to govern his subjects.

Uncle Oscar pointed out that the Sabbath commandment, alone among the 10, identifies God as Creator and asserts His authority because of His creative acts. The Sabbath is like a king's seal, Uncle Oscar explained. The Creator uses it as the stamp of His authority. "I made you," He says, "and I know what is best for you." And "you," said Uncle Oscar, doesn't mean just the Jew. Jesus said the Sabbath "was made for man" (Mark 2:27). Most every Christian, he said, will tell you that a Christian cannot, in good conscience, violate nine of the Ten Commandments. The exception, of course, is the fourth.

So important are the principles of this law that Jesus died for our disobeying them (see Romans 3:23 and 6:23). The good news—the "gospel"—is that Jesus let men execute Him to spare us the death penalty. One cannot, therefore, separate the Ten Commandments and the gospel. If the law could have been done away with, Jesus would not have had to die. If the gospel were dispensed with, all the world would perish. So both gospel and law offer reasons to acknowledge God's authority as Creator and as Redeemer.

## The Sabbath as a Test of Loyalty

Uncle Oscar argued that if one accepts the premise that God, as Creator, has the right to instruct His creation how to live happily, then one should accept the corollary—it is His children's loving obligation to fly the flag of their loyalty, the Sabbath, over the embassy of their hearts. In fact, Jesus made observance of all His commandments a love test: "If you love Me," He told His disciples, "keep My commandments" (John 14:15, NKJV). He made obedience a test of friendship: "Ye are my friends, if ye do whatsoever I command you" (John 15:14). And He emphatically linked obedience with true worship: "It is of no use for them [religious leaders] to worship me, because they teach man-made rules as though they were my laws! You put aside God's command and obey the teachings of men" (Mark 7:7, 8, TEV).

How does the Sabbath become a test of God's authority and our loyalty? I remember Uncle Oscar referring to Daniel 7:25, which speaks of a power that would arise and "think to change times and laws." If I'd had a part in such a challenge to God's authority, I surely wouldn't want to admit it. But the incredible fact is that church spokespersons, both Protestant and Catholic, admit that no Bible warrant exists for discarding the Sabbath for Sunday. On the basics, they agree how it happened. Here's one explanation, typical of many from Catholic sources:

"Nowhere in the Bible do we find that Christ or the apostles ordered that the Sabbath be changed from Saturday to Sunday. We have the commandment of God . . . to keep holy the Sabbath day, that is the seventh day of the week, Saturday. Today most Christians keep Sunday because it has been revealed to us by the [Roman Catholic] church outside the Bible" (*Catholic Virginian,* Oct. 3, 1947). Other Catholic sources, including catechisms, chide Protestants for accepting a change made by the church and not authorized in Scripture.

Says Peter Heylyn, an Episcopal historian: "Take which you will, either the Fathers or the moderns, and we shall find no Lord's day instituted by any apostolic mandate, no Sabbath set on foot by them upon the first day of the week" (*History of the Sabbath,* p. 410).

Augustus Neander wrote, in *The History of the Christian Religion and Church,* "The festival of Sunday, like all other festivals, was always only a human ordinance."

Recently the Catholic Church, likely for reasons of ecumenism, has changed the party line: it now claims the Bible reveals that it is God Himself who changed the Sabbath to Sunday. But Jesus said of those who sought to alter His commandments: "You have let go of the commands of God and are holding on to the traditions of men" (Mark 7:8, NIV). We can only hope that some Protestants will not forget why "protest" is part of their name.

How did the change come about?

First, Jewish revolts against the Romans, in the first

and second centuries, made being Jewish perilous. Because the early Christians kept the Sabbath, the Romans misidentified them as Jews. Worshipping with Romans on the "venerable day of the sun" was much safer than worshipping with the Jews on Sabbath.

Then, after the apostles and their followers died, church leaders decided to play God. As the mark of their authority, they substituted a new day for worship. The change took place gradually, beginning with a yearly commemoration of Jesus' resurrection. With the encouragement of the bishop of Rome, Sunday became a weekly celebration.

In the fourth century, along came the Roman emperor Constantine, an astute politician who converted to Christianity, decreed that pagan and Christian alike worship on Sunday, and enacted the world's first civil Sunday law. The emerging Papacy furthered the apostasy, and finally, through alliance with the state, persecuted those followers of Jesus who, in regard to Sabbathkeeping and other biblical practices, insisted on giving loyalty to the Creator instead of His creatures.

This much is conclusive: First, that the seventh day is the Sabbath; second, that worship on Sunday developed slowly as the church slid into apostasy; third, that the Bible nowhere authorizes the change to Sunday. In fact, the issue in the New Testament is never which day is the Sabbath; rather, it is how the Sabbath is to be kept.

## The Sabbath Defines
### Who Is to Be Worshipped and How

Scripture reveals—and Uncle Oscar turned to the verses—that it has ever been Lucifer's ambition to mount the throne of God and usurp the worship due only to Him. "You have said in your heart," says the

Reader of hearts, "I will ascend into heaven, I will exalt my throne above the stars of God; . . . I will be like the Most High!" (Isaiah 14:13, 14, NKJV).

The controversy that rent the fabric of heaven itself began when one of God's creatures developed a passion to be worshipped. And it continued on earth as the rebel leader, Lucifer, was cast out of heaven with his seduced legions. The Bible reveals a critical skirmish on a wilderness battlefield, when Lucifer, masquerading as an agent of God, confronts Jesus with three temptations. Transparent in the account is the rebel's continued determination to be worshipped.

"The devil took him [Jesus] to a very high mountain, and from there showed him all the kingdoms of the world and their magnificence. 'Everything there I will give you,' he said to him, 'if you will fall down and worship me'" (Matthew 4:8, 9, Phillips).

"'Away with you, Satan!' replied Jesus, 'the scripture says, Thou shalt worship the Lord thy God, and him only shalt thou serve.' Then the devil left him" (verses 10, 11, Phillips).

His craving for worship undiminished, the devil left, determined to secure from the church the obeisance that he could not get from its Founder in the wilderness. We're indebted to John the revelator for an intelligence report on where Satan went from his defeat at the hands of Christ. Chapter 12 pictures Satan coming from his wilderness defeat to make war plans (verse 17) against those who, in the end-time, persist in loyally keeping the commandments of God.

Satan's fury is focused particularly on the Sabbath commandment, because above all others it stands as an impediment to his ambition to be worshipped. In chapter 13 John reveals the devil's strategy against the church. In every confrontation—verses 4, 8, 12, 15—the issue is worship. By deceit, persecution, wonders, signs, miracles, Satan attempts to gain the worship of all humanity. And in a final, desperate gambit, just as he appeared to Christ in the wilderness as an angel from heaven, he shall appear in the end-time to humanity as the Messiah!

In Revelation 14 John commissions Christ's last legion to counter the devil, not with miracles, but with God's Word. Foremost is the preaching of the everlasting gospel to "them that dwell on the earth, and to every nation, and kindred, and tongue, and people" (verse 6). The message is urgent because, as John reveals, "the hour of God's judgment is come."

In response, God's loyal followers "reverence" God and "give Him glory" by inviting Him to reveal Himself to the world through them! And they, in turn, call the world to "worship him that made heaven, and earth, and the sea, and the fountains of waters" (verse 7). Where are these words found elsewhere in the Bible? *In the Sabbath commandment!* What is the issue? *Worship. The world must be in terrible danger of worshipping a counterfeit god on his counterfeit day!* Once again, at world's end, the paramount issue in the great controversy between Christ and Satan shall be who is to be worshipped. And the mark of discipleship shall be observance of the Sabbath—*God's* Sabbath, the seventh day of the week.

As these truths confronted me during my college years, I faced a choice, just as Uncle Oscar had, just as millions throughout the centuries have, and just as millions more shall: Either to join a people who "keep the commandments of God, and have the testimony of Jesus Christ" (Revelation 12:17), or to join those who claim that the church rather than Scripture is the definer of God's will.

I should not ignore those earnest Christians who faithfully observe Sunday in honor of Christ's resurrection. Let me pause a gentle moment on their case. Unfortunately for the resurrection hypothesis, no scripture transfers God's seal of authority to Sunday. Instead, Jesus warned emphatically against attempting to change His commandments. Note Matthew 5:17-19: "You must not think that I have come to abolish the Law or the Prophets; I have not come to abolish them but to complete them. Indeed, I assure you that, while Heaven and earth last, the Law will not lose a single dot or comma until its purpose is complete. This means that whoever now relaxes one of the least of these commandments and teaches men to do the same will himself be called least in the kingdom of Heaven. But whoever teaches and practices them will be called great in the kingdom of Heaven" (Phillips).

No, I don't agree with those who keep Sunday because Jesus was resurrected on that day. The New Testament gives us another ordinance by which we are to celebrate Christ's death, burial, and resurrection. It is called baptism, and you can read about it in Romans 6. Through baptism, Paul tells us, we figuratively go down into the grave with Jesus and come up as participants in His resurrection.

Those who commemorate the resurrection by Sunday worship are misguided, but one must say two things in their behalf: They do make more sense than those who argue that Sundaykeeping is rooted in the fourth commandment. Furthermore, many Sunday-keeping Christians are trusting fully in Christ for their salvation; they are keeping the wrong day for the right reason. And what of seventh-day Sabbathkeepers who believe their Sabbathkeeping will save them? They are keeping the right day for the wrong reason.

My decision, which I arrived at during my college years, involved acknowledging God's authority and His right to my allegiance. I asked myself: "When I stand in judgment before my Creator, which argument would I rather advance in my defense: The church said or the Bible said?" My answer, I felt, was eminently reasonable.

Unfortunately, it was also eminently insufficient. We have too many church members who are not really Sabbathkeepers. To truly rest on the Sabbath day involves more than knowing Saturday is the Sabbath; that the Sabbath is a symbol of God's authority, and further, the test of our loyalty. One can believe all this and be lost. Our right to the kingdom depends today on what it always has—perfect obedience to God's will. And we are no more capable of producing that today than we have ever been, for "all have sinned, and come short of the glory of God" (Romans 3:23). Salvation is the "free gift" of "eternal life through Jesus Christ our Lord" (Romans 6:23, Phillips). When Jesus invites us to rest, or "Sabbath" with Him, He invites us not only to cease from our physical labors but to rest trustfully in His finished work of redemption.

My high school sweetheart and I used to stop at the home of my uncle Stanley Peterson and his wife, Sylvia, on our way to dances in the old Norse Hall on Puget Island, Washington. Never did Aunt Sylvia get on my case. When my grandmother Hegstad died, I went to Sylvia with questions about life and death and whether there really was a God. She urged me to find my answers at a Christian college. In some way I still cannot explain, the Holy Spirit gently urged me to follow her counsel. I remember her for two graces: Her assurance of redemption and her kindness to everyone. Both she and Uncle Oscar knew they were children of the King. They loved Jesus for taking their sins to Calvary and stamping their account "Paid in full." I've got a mental picture of them walking hand in hand with their families in the new earth, beside the river of life. They treasured God's assurance that no one could snatch them out of God's hand (John 10:28). Each Sabbath pointed them to a finished creation and a finished redemption.

From them I learned that only when one sees the Sabbath in the context of the gospel, only when one thrills to the assurance of a finished work at Calvary, can one truly enjoy Sabbath rest. It was this understanding that sent Sylvia out on missions of mercy as a gracious witness for her Savior. To her, the essence of Sabbathkeeping was people to love rather than rules to obey (see Luke 13:12-16).

Come with me, then, to her home on Puget Island for a brief remembrance of her works of mercy. The Peterson home was open to all. She and Stanley used to take in problem children that the state social agencies couldn't help. They loved them, worked them on the farm, and in several instances, educated them along with their own three daughters. Sylvia was in charge of outreach to the less fortunate in the community around a little Adventist church just across the bridge in Cathlamet, Washington. If anyone for 20 miles up and down the Columbia was sick, Aunt Sylvia was there with a hot meal, a good book, or even a vacuum cleaner. In her Sabbath ministry—and it extended to the six other days as well—Aunt Sylvia was fulfilling the mission of Jesus, as forecast by the gospel prophet Isaiah: "to loose the chains of injustice and untie the cords of the yoke, to set the oppressed free and break every yoke. . . . To share your food with the hungry and to provide the poor wanderer with shelter—when you see the naked, to clothe him, and not to turn away from your own flesh and blood" (Isaiah 58:6, 7, NIV).

That, she told me, was the way you bring

"Sabbath" to people. As Christ's ministry documents, deeds of mercy and healing and kindness and the Sabbath go together, because, since sin came on the scene, the Sabbath speaks to us of restoration. That's why Jesus performed many of His restorative miracles on the Sabbath. That's why Aunt Sylvia spent her Sabbaths wiping tears and sweeping sadness right out the door.

When she died, most of Puget Island and Cathlamet, population 635, came to the funeral, along with people from up and down both the Oregon and Washington sides of the Columbia. They couldn't all get into the little church; they filled the lawn and looked and listened through the church windows. They all loved Aunt Sylvia, and when they thought of her, they were celebrating what God has ever intended the Sabbath to be.

Both Aunt Sylvia and Uncle Oscar contributed to my decision to commit my life to Christ and to ministry in a church that treasures the commandments of God and the faith of Jesus. Someday soon I plan to visit both of them in that land where "all things bright and beautiful" will be ours again. "For as the new heavens and the new earth, which I will make, shall remain before me, saith the Lord, so shall your seed and your name remain. And it shall come to pass, that from one new moon to another, and from one sabbath to another, shall all flesh come to worship before me, saith the Lord" (Isaiah 66:22, 23).

When I meet Uncle Oscar and Aunt Sylvia I'm going ask them, "What made you determine to honor the Sabbath?" And they'll probably say:

"We honored the Sabbath as a symbol of God's authority, as the test of loyalty, and as the definer of who was to be worshipped and how. We honored it because of its assurance of Christ's perfect and finished redemptive work, and because it pointed us to the restoration of all things bright and beautiful.

"We found the Sabbath to be a unique and beautiful weekly reminder of God's love. And we decided that too many people had paid for it with their blood for us to demean it by choosing another day, a day that has come to symbolize rebellion against God's holy law."

If you're comfortable with the Sabbath as the Bible teaches it, and as Uncle Oscar and Aunt Sylvia lived it, I'd like to invite you to join the Lord of the Sabbath in Sabbath services not only down here but up there, for, as Isaiah promised, "It shall come to pass, that from . . . one sabbath to another, all flesh shall come to worship before me, saith the Lord."

## Chapter 11

# AT THE CROSSROADS

A doniram Judson was raised in the New England of a century and a half ago. As a young man he decided that he didn't want to be a Christian. But obedient to his preacher father, he entered what is now Brown University at age 16. That may seem young for college, but Adoniram was reading at 3 and was a Latin scholar at 6. At college Adoniram became a close friend of Jacob Eames, a brilliant youth who rejected all revealed religion.

Under the influence of their friendship and numerous discussions, Adoniram's belief structure collapsed. At 19 he graduated as valedictorian of his class and returned to his home in Plymouth. But his soul was in revolt; he felt like a hypocrite when he knelt for prayers. Finally he decided to leave for New York City to write for the theater. His parents were distressed. His father asked him to stay and study to be a minister. Goaded too far, Adoniram flung out the words "Your church is no longer mine. The Bible is nothing but the works of man. Even Jesus was only a man."

His father tried logic but couldn't cope with his son's brilliant mind. His mother, weeping, pursued him from room to room; when sobs didn't avail, she turned to prayer. For six days Adoniram endured the assault; then he mounted his horse, put on his black hat, and rode away—to freedom!

In New York City Judson lived as a restless vagabond, finding lodging where he could and bilking landlords when he couldn't. Finally, disgruntled and filled with a strange unease, he rode away to any-where. He had won his freedom. One night he stopped at a small village inn. "Only one room is avail-able," the landlord told him. "You might not sleep well. The young man in the next room is dying."

Adoniram felt he could sleep through anything. But sleep wouldn't come. He could hear noises from the adjacent room—footsteps coming and going, a board creaking; low voices, a groan or gasp. Death didn't bother him much. It was common in the New England of his day.

What disturbed him was the thought that the man in the next room might not be prepared for death. Was he himself? How would he face death? he won-dered. His flesh crawled as he thought of the coldness of the grave, the weight of the soil, the crumbling of bones. Terror filled his heart, but with it all, he felt shame. He could imagine Jacob Eames' laughter, and felt embarrassed at this pang of conscience.

The next morning, as he was leaving, Adoniram asked, "How's the young man in the next room?"

"Dead," the landlord replied. Dead. The word had a heavy finality.

For an instant the fear of the night flowed back. As he started for the door, he paused, turned back, and asked: "Do you know who he was?"

"Yes. A young man from the college in Providence. Name was Eames. Jacob Eames."

It was hours before Adoniram was able to leave the inn. Later, as he found himself riding along the road, one word tolled like a bell in his mind: Lost!

Lost! Lost! Jacob Eames was lost—lost to his friends, lost to the world, lost to the future. Lost as a puff of air. But suppose the Bible were true. Then Eames was eternally lost. That a grave could open in a country inn and swallow up his dearest friend while he slept next door—this could not be coincidence! Had he failed the chance to minister to Eames? Had his father's God led him to the inn? He reined in his horse and sat stiff and silent in the saddle for what seemed forever. He was at a crossroad. Where should he go? At last he turned his horse about and headed back toward Plymouth and home.

The road he chose led to much more than Plymouth. It led to agonies of soul, to further study; to full surrender to God and to His Son, Jesus Christ. It led to the mission field—Adoniram Judson became the first missionary to Burma. The first to translate the Scriptures into Burmese. It was a road that led to the loss of two wives, to torture, to suffering, but never again to the agony of soul he had felt that day in the village inn.

Prodigals. The world is full of them. I've been one. Have you?

Let me introduce another.

This second prodigal's story is found in the most famous of all Christ's parables, likely dating to the last two months of His ministry. The parable begins with the simple words "A certain man had two sons" (Luke 15:11). The youngest is the bad guy. In Jesus' parable he represents the black sheep of the family—the publicans and other sinners of the day. The older brother represents the upright folks—the scribes and Pharisees. It seems that dishonest tax collectors and other notorious sinners often came to hear Jesus preach. And sometimes Jesus would share a meal with them. In fact, He gave every appearance of liking them! And that, the religious leaders couldn't stomach. So Jesus gave three parables: of the lost sheep, the lost coin, and the lost son. Each in a subtle way touches a dimension of lostness.

The sheep was lost through its own carelessness.

The coin was lost through someone else's carelessness.

The prodigal was lost through his own defiance.

All three parables tell us something about God's yearning for lost sinners. And the great news is this: "There is joy in the presence of the angels of God over one sinner who repents (verse 10, NKJV).

But let's not take anything for granted. Let's pick up the story of the prodigal. And let's put a black hat on him!

You can almost see the audience leaning closer as Jesus begins His parable: "A man had two sons. When the younger told his father, 'I want my share of your estate now, instead of waiting until you die!' his father agreed to divide his wealth between his sons" (verses 11, 12, TLB).

The older son is a story in himself. He wears the white hat in the family—and some of you, from under your black hats, know how irritating that kind of brother or sister or wife or husband or parent or neighbor or classmate can be. Get around a white hat, and yours always seems a little blacker than it really is. It's even worse when the good guy is the one you suspect to be the family favorite.

Let's draw on our imaginations to fill in the story. One day father comes home to a confrontation with his younger son, who reacts: "Dad," he says, "this country life may be OK for you and mom and my white-hatted brother, but as for me, I want to live! I'm tired of sitting around watching *Wheel of Fortune* and *Who Wants to Be a Millionaire*. That's kid stuff! You only live once, you know!"

Notice that not one thing in the prodigal's complaints constitutes a legitimate gripe, a real reason for leaving. Instead, he has every reason to stay. His father is an important man in the community. He's wealthy. They have servants. Their home is palatial—I picture it with a recreation room, antique furniture, and original oils by Picasso. Certainly the father is not obligated to give the son a part of the estate. In fact, the son's asking for it is a slap in his father's face, a slur on his business ability, a rejection of his authority. But the father agrees, as parents sometimes do, even when they think it to be unwise. Land is sold, other assets converted to cash, and the Great Leaving comes. The prodigal, you can be sure, gets the beast of burden that is the Bugatti Veyron 16.4 of his day. Leave the Hyundai for big brother.

The story doesn't tell us the son's destination, other than saying it is a "far country." But give a teenager wheels and money and his freedom, and he won't head for Iowa to plant corn; he heads for Vegas to plant tares. It's heady stuff, this freedom; he's going to really live! Wine, women, song—maybe a bit of gambling at the Las Vegas Hilton—all the time his brother will be pitching hay and scratching! So the prodigal drives off, leaving just a whiff of Versace to mix with the burnt rubber. His radio isn't tuned to the *Quiet Hour,* you can be sure, and he has a joint between his lips before he's out of the driveway.

There's something wise about Jesus' saying only that the prodigal's destination is a far country. It leaves us free to write in our own fantasies. . . . And maybe in speaking of a far country, Jesus has something more in mind than geography. For a man can live in his own far country at home—in the quietness of his study and the presence of his laptop: women and song at the press of a button. And yes, a woman can find her own far country there.

To every prodigal there comes an awakening. A few days, a few weeks, a few months. The prodigal of our story soon wasted all his money on parties and prostitutes, as the record says, and "about the time his money was gone a great famine swept over the land, and he began to starve" (verse 14, TLB).

I visited a modern prodigal a few months ago in a Western city, where I once pastored. He is now a drunkard, a bully, and a con man. He entertains the ultimate illusion—he has come to believe himself. His mother was a member of my church. He had been raised a Christian, but he got in with the wrong crowd. He put on a black hat. Went to his own far country. Had to marry his girlfriend. Dropped out of school, got a job, and began to buy his wife nice things. She loved nice things. Expensive clothes. Expensive perfumes. Expensive furniture. She loved it all. And he loved her.

One day the police picked him up. It seems that he paid for something with a bad check. The bartender remembered his face, and this time he spent six months in prison. His wife and little boy waited for him. But she still loved nice things. And he still loved her. And he still could write.

I tried to help John. I got him another chance. But John didn't like preachers, and we seldom went to the same places for recreation. He was seeking bonded spirits—100 proof—and I could offer only the Spirit that frees men and women from bonds. Soon after, his wife divorced him. When he finally came to me, it was too late. The police were considerate. They released him to me so that I could drive him to the Idaho State Penitentiary.

Along the way we stopped at his parents' little

white-frame house on a quiet side street. His mother kissed him and cried. His father hugged him—I can still see his old hands shaking. Then I drove John to his former wife's house, where he had two little children to wave goodbye to. Across the years, I can see them yet—their mother behind them in the doorway . . . mixed emotions fighting for possession of her face; the two children, sad-eyed, waving, calling, "Goodbye, Daddy! Goodbye . . ."

There's a terrible finality sometimes in goodbyes. And sin leads to so many of them. And it's all so senseless, so unnecessary. So illusionary.

One morning the prodigal of Jesus' parable awakened without a shekel to his name, and with considerably fewer illusions than before. Too many prodigals at such a time go on the Internet and sweet-talk Dad. Or fasten themselves, parasitically, to acquaintances. But this prodigal, the son of a prominent Jew, got a job feeding pigs. Shame. Humiliation.

Then one day pig man leaned on his shovel by the manure pile and began to reflect. "At home even the hired men have plenty of food, and here I am, dying of hunger!"

The significant phrase in the story is "when he came to himself." You see, sin doesn't make sense, however attractively it is packaged. It's delusive. Paul writes that sinners live "in a world of shadows" (Ephesians 4:18, Phillips). And he warns again of "the delusive glamour of sin" (Hebrews 3:13, Phillips). A delusion the wise person learns to recognize as he or she goes through life is that one can give only part of himself or herself to God, and that's called discipleship. Not so. It's all or nothing at all.

We're now at the crisis of the Bible story. To this point, the prodigal has been going away from home, away from his father's house. But now he pauses, and reflects on home and its values. Many prodigals come to such a time of assessment and go on to oblivion. They pause from their sinning; they dream of doing better. But they make no determined decision. They use their wishbone rather than their backbone. They don't surrender their will to God.

Everything depends on this moment. What will the prodigal do? The answer comes: "I will go home to my father." The original language reflects determination: "I am determined to go to my father. I will!"

You don't have a will? It's worn out? Then try your "won't." That may help keep you from turning your back on your heavenly Father in the first place. Then work on the "will," and let the omnipotent will of Jesus unite with yours and put steel in your determination.

Sin is slippery. Sneaky. It slips up on us. Pause and consider: What are you doing now that you would not have done a year ago? The conscience must be kept warm and fresh with the love of God. Otherwise, you will awaken someday to find yourself doing what you had come to abhor, and that without a pang of conscience.

Change does not come suddenly. Apostasy is not announced by trumpets. Change takes place imperceptibly, in thousands of tiny, almost unnoticed ways, through infinitesimal shifts of emphasis, now here, now there, until the thing is done. Then, and only then, we who have lived unconsciously through the process reach the point where, suddenly, as though empowered to recognize it for the first time, we can perceive the difference the years have made.

What does the prodigal say?

"I will go home to my father and say, 'Father, I have sinned against both heaven and you, and am no longer worthy of being called your son. Please take me on as a hired hand'" (Luke 15:19, TLB).

Notice that as soon as the decision is made, the prodigal confesses. Thus it must be with everyone who starts over. I think of a man I baptized. After a few months his experience began to deteriorate. He became critical of everyone in the church. One day I went to him. "Curt, what is it? There is something wrong. What can I do to help?"

Soon the story was out. He had taken something from an abandoned government building before his baptism. The Lord brought his transgression into his mind, with the conviction that he should make the matter right. But he was afraid that confession could cost him his job with the government—and perhaps more. Before I left, he made his decision: "I will." He packaged the items and sent them back. One day at work an FBI agent tapped him on the shoulder. But after a little chat the agent left, and the matter was closed. When Jesus asks us to confess and to restore, He does not leave us to do it alone. He works to soften hearts, to prepare the way for us.

As we pick up the story of the prodigal we find him a lonely hitchhiker headed home. No Versace now—though after months with the pigs, he could use some. There are scars without and within. Scars that will always remain. Sin doesn't leave us as it found us.

I've wondered whether the prodigal rehearsed a few excuses on the way home: "It was this way. . . . You know what a prig my brother is. . . . And if only you had not been so demanding. . . . All those rules . . ."

And then one day the prodigal finds himself in the old neighborhood. He can see the house—far up on a hill. Panic sweeps over him. What if his brother sees him dressed like this? What if his father won't accept him?

At this point the perspective of the story

changes. Jesus puts us in the living room with the father. Could he have known—or was it just hope that made him pause by the window and look longingly down the driveway, as he had so many times in the lonely months? There's a beautiful touch to the story here: Jesus emphasizes that the father saw his son "while he was a great way off." I can see the father look through the window, move to the door, step out onto the porch. He wants to believe, but the disappointments have been so many. Still, the way he walks . . . the way he carries his shoulders . . . Can it be?

Oh, yes! It's his son!

"While he was still a long distance away, his father saw him coming, and was filled with loving pity and ran and embraced him and kissed him. His son said to him, 'Father, I have sinned against heaven and you, and am not worthy of being called your son'" (verses 20, 21, TLB).

His father turns to a servant. "Quick! Bring the finest robe in the house and put it on him!" The robe was the emblem of sonhood. For us, it typifies the robe of righteousness our heavenly Father offers us. "[Bring] a jeweled ring for his finger." The ring was a symbol of authority and power. "And shoes" (verse 22, TLB). Servants didn't have shoes. Putting on the shoes meant that freedom was restored. As the old spiritual puts it: "all God's chil'n got shoes!"

Ironic, isn't it? For the first time since the prodigal left to seek his freedom, he is really free—free within the happiness of his father's house. Free within the family rules. And so it is with us. We are truly free only when we submit to the authority of our heavenly Parent. That's why Jesus called the Ten Commandments the "law of liberty." Only in obedience to that law are we truly free—

Free from the slavery of sin.
Free from the lash of lust.
Free from the shackles of habit.
Free from the tyranny of appetite.
Free from the bondage of death.

There is, however, one thing the prodigal son is not freed from: the resentment of his brother. I think I know how Jesus might have wished to tell the story: "One day the older brother saw his father grieving, and he said, 'Father, let me go and look for my brother. And when I find him, I'll put my arm over his shoulder, and I'll tell him that we want him to come home'." But the story doesn't go that way. He says to his father: "All these years I've worked hard for you and never once refused to do a single thing you told me to do; and in all that time you never gave me even one young goat for a feast with my friends. Yet when this son of yours comes back after spending your money on prostitutes, you celebrate by killing the finest calf we have on the place to give him a feast!" (verses 29, 30, TLB).

The older son is angry: he's worn his white hat with pride; he's worked for his status in the family, and like most people who work for their status, he just can't see his brother getting off so easy. If the elder brother had his way, his father's "other son" would be required to give a full report of his peccadilloes—names, dates, and places. And then he'd be put on probation for a few years until he'd proved himself. Is that the way God runs His forgiveness bureau?

Remember what He said to the woman caught in adultery? "Woman, I don't condemn you; go your way and sin no more." He extends the same grace to the returned prodigal. And to you. And to me.

The lost is found. He who was dead in sin has

come back to life. By this parable, Jesus reinforces the point of the parables of the lost sheep and the lost coin: you can expect a loving and gracious reception when you repent and come home.

But beautiful as the parable is—and it's more the story of the gracious Father than of the prodigal son—it still falls far short of fully revealing God's outreaching love. Create a hundred parables, and you're still left breathless at the unseen dimensions of God's love. The theologian Helmut Thielicke has said: "Christ is the very voice of the father's heart that overtakes us in the far country and tells us that incredibly joyful news, 'You can come home. Come home.'"

In a sense the parable echoes God's testimony of love through Hosea:

"When Israel was a child I loved him as a son and brought him out of Egypt. But the more I called to him, the more he rebelled, sacrificing to Baal and burning incense to idols. I trained him from infancy, I taught him to walk, I held him in my arms. But he doesn't know or even care that it was I who raised him. . . .

"Oh, how can I give you up, my Ephraim? How can I let you go? . . . My heart cries out within me; how I long to help you! No, I will not punish you as much as my fierce anger tells me to. . . . For I am God and not man; I am the Holy One living among you, and I did not come to destroy" (Hosea 11:1-9, TLB).

No, Jesus did not come to condemn the world, but that the world through Him might be saved. He came to seek and to save the lost. The lost world, the lost coin, the lost sheep, the lost son. Love wrapped itself in the likeness of our sinful flesh: God became one with us. And by so doing, His intention was to confront a world of prodigals:

Those dissatisfied.

Those leaving home.

Those eating husks.

Those desiring to return.

Those breathing the words "I will." And yes, even the elder brother who refused to come to the feast!

To all He says: Let Me tell you something. I can't bear the thought of going through eternity without you. You see, you are important to Me. Before the world began, you were part of My plan. I chose you. I cut you out of the herd and branded you as My own. I love you—just as you are right now. Right now, I love you. Right now.

And here, you see, we come to another prodigal's story. Perhaps it's yours. Only you know where you are in that far country.

Only you.

A rich businessman in Chicago had a lovely wife. Her beauty was not of looks alone, but of character— strong, true. Friends often came to their house; it seemed never to be without the sound of laughter.

But one day the young wife became ill, with a terrible fever. And when it had passed, her eyes were empty. Her memory destroyed. Her husband took her from specialist to specialist. He spent a fortune in the greatest medical clinics of the land. He sold their home and business, spending every dollar in a futile attempt to help her.

Finally one lone hope remained. A world-renowned specialist said that there was a chance she would regain her memory if she could be taken back to the scenes of her childhood. So the husband took her to the bluegrass country of Kentucky, where they had lived as children. Hand in hand they wandered down the paths they had known long ago.

But it was all unavailing. And so they returned to Chicago, to a small house he had rented. The business was gone, their bank account emptied. He bowed hi.

head in his hands and wept. Hour after hour he sat, despondent, hopeless. Ten o'clock. Eleven o'clock. Twelve. His wife slept. He watched the gentle movement of her breathing. One, two, three, four o'clock . . .

The sun turned the sky to molten orange. Five o'clock. The light shone on her hair, shimmering, caressing. Six o'clock. Seven. Eight. She stirred. He watched as she moved, stretched. Her eyes opened. Slowly a puzzled frown creased her brow. She turned her head toward him. "John." She spoke his name for the first time in months. "John!"

She reached uncertainly for his hand. "John! It seems that I've been on a long, sad journey. Oh, John, where have you been?"

Throwing himself to his knees beside the bed, he crushed her to him, crying, "Oh, my darling, I've been waiting for you."

One who emptied heaven for us reaches out in anguish to cry, "Oh, how can I give you up! Please come home from your wanderings, home from your sin, home from your far country.

"I'm waiting for you!"